Wildy Practice

G000160832

Change of Name

The Law & Practice

by

Nasreen Pearce

Third edition

Wildy, Simmonds and Hill Publishing

First published in Great Britain 2010 by Wildy, Simmonds & Hill Publishing

Website: www.wildy.com

Nasreen Pearce

Change of Name (Wildy Practice Guides series)

ISBN 9780854900442

Printed and bound in Great Britain

Preface

The aim of this short handbook is to provide a simple, practical and straightforward guide to the law and procedure relating to changing a person's name. A concise statement of the law is provided and, in respect of a change in a child's name, the application of the general principles under the Children Act 1989 are outlined and illustrated by case law. Where appropriate, a procedural guide to the making of an application to the court is set out. This edition also briefly considers the relevant provisions of the Adoption and Children Act 2002, which is now in force, changes brought about by the Human Fertilisation and Embryology Act 2008, issues affecting those in same sex relationships and the impact of the Civil Partnership Act 2004.Reference is also made where appropriate to the Gender Recognition Act 2004.

The book is not intended to be a definitive text and, for example, does not deal with the specialised law relating to bodies corporate or to ships. Although some instances of the requirements of professional organisations have been included, the ground covered is not exhaustive. In all such cases, reference should be made to the appropriate professional body for its specific requirements.

Finally, I would like to express my gratitude to the Human Fertilisation and Embryology Authority for providing information regarding the new forms.

Nasreen Pearce

September 2009

Contents

1 Introduction

1.1 Background

What's in a name? It is a question often asked. A name, and particularly a surname, may not carry any significance other than as a means of identifying a person. It may on the other hand, be an important label, indicating a person's relationship with another, or signifying biological and genealogical identity and origin. In many communities a surname of a person is very significant as it links the person to a particular tribe or clan. Such connections may, for a multitude of reasons, lead a person to change his or her name or that of a child. A change of name could also be a way of confirming a change of status or resolving an embarrassment. A person may change his/her name to disassociate himself or herself from past events or circumstances or from a relationship which would be best forgotten.

A person may wish to assume a new forename and surname by reason of necessity and as a means of self protection of himself/herself and his/her family from reprisals, vendetta or persecution. For example it is not uncommon for a witness or informant or even a defendant in a high profile case to assume a new name and identity to avoid being identified.

With the rise in divorce, and the increase in single parent families and step-families, there may be numerous motives for a person to change his or her name and that of a child. A mother may wish to change her child's name following separation from the father of the child to avoid embarrassment because she has reverted to her maiden name, or because she is in a new relationship and has assumed the name of her new partner.

Where a new relationship involves step-children or siblings the reason for changing a name or names may be to give all the children a uniform identity and thus secure and stabilise the 'family' as a single unit. Where a former relationship has been an unhappy one and the breakdown has been acrimonious, a name change may be seen not only as a means of cutting the ties but also as severance from past grievances.

The provisions contained in the Gender Recognition Act 2004, which provides transsexual persons legal recognition in their acquired gender, necessarily lead to a change of name and an appropriate entry on the Gender Recognition Register.

As a result of the Civil Partnership Act 2004, same sex couples have a right to enter into a civil partnership which is recognised in law and given similar status as that of marriage. Such a relationship may also give rise to a wish by one partner to assume the name of his/her partner or for both partners to change their names to a double-barrelled name. Male couples in a relationship may father a child. When s 54 of the HFEA 2008 comes into force (expected April 2010) they will be able to jointly assume parenthood by obtaining a parental order. They may then wish to change the child's name. Same sex couples with a child may also want to change a child's name by agreement or seek an order for a change of name for similar reasons as heterosexual couples.

Whatever the reason may be for a person wishing to change his/her name or that of his or her child, it is important to the person making the change to ensure that it has legal effect. It is often believed that to make a change involves a great deal of trouble, expense and complicated legal process. Depending on the circumstances of the individual case, the change may be effected quite simply, and at no cost or at very little expense. In the case of an adult the law does not prescribe any limitations on a person's right to change his or her name. A name is a means of identification and the law is concerned only with the question of whether the assumed name is the one by which the person has come to be known and identified. Provided that, in adopting a new name, a person does not thereby intend to deceive or defraud another, that person may change his or her name or surname; add names to the original name or surname; substitute a name or names; or simply re-arrange the order of names.

A person acquires his or her original name when that name is registered at birth under the Births and Deaths Registration Act 1953 (1953 Act) as amended. Provision is made in that Act, and in the Family Law Reform Act 1987, for re-registration in certain circumstances (see Chapter 2).

A person may have had a forename conferred at baptism. There is some uncertainty as to whether or not a Christian name may be changed, and if so, how. In *R v Smith* (1865) 4 F & F 1099, it was observed that a Christian name may not be changed. In *Re Parrott* [1946] Ch 183, Vaisey J said that there may be only three ways in which a Christian name may be changed (see 5.6). It is, however, possible to change a Christian name on confirmation (again, see 5.6).

On marriage, a woman usually chooses to take the surname of her husband. However, there is no legal requirement for her to abandon her maiden name and assume her husband's surname (see 5.5).

An adult may change his name simply by becoming known by the assumed name by reputation, advertising the fact that he has relinquished his former name and confirming the name by which he desires to be known. A statutory declaration to that effect may also be made (see 5.1 to 5.4).

To avoid confusion and doubt, the most common formal method of changing a name is by deed poll. This is dealt with in Chapter 4. Other more complicated and expensive methods include a change by an Act of Parliament and royal licence (see Chapter 5).

Those who follow a profession may change their names like any other individual, but the governing body or organisation of the profession of which the person is a member may require compliance with the requirements of their rules and regulations, or may require formal evidence of a change of name before recognising the change or altering the register, if a register is kept (see Chapter 6).

Changing the name of a child who is under the age of 16 years can be simple if the parents agree. If they do not, legal proceedings may need to be issued as there are restrictions on effecting a change of name of a child (see Chapter 3).

Where a child is to be adopted and the proposed adopters wish the child to be known by a different name, the child's name may be changed provided the prescribed procedure is followed (see 3.7.2 and 5.10).

An alien too may change his name, but there are certain restrictions. These are discussed at 4.2.

Thus, save in respect of a name given in baptism, and except for the restrictions imposed on changing the name of a child and of an alien, there are no legal objections or bars to a person's changing his or her name.

2 Registration and Re-registration under the Births and Deaths Registration Act 1953

2.1 Registration of live births

Section 1 of the Births and Deaths Registration Act 1953 as amended (1953 Act) provides that the birth of every child born in England and Wales must be registered by the Registrar of Births and Deaths for the sub-district in which the child was born, by entering in a register kept for that sub-district such particulars concerning the birth of the child as are required by regulations made under the Act.

By virtue of reg 7 of the Registration of Births and Deaths Regulations 1987 (SI 1987/2088) (1987 Regulations) as amended by the Registration of Births and Deaths (Amendment) Regulations 1994 (SI 1994/1948) and the Registration of Births and Deaths (Amendment) (England and Wales) Regulations 2009 (SI 2009/2165), the particulars required to be registered under s 5 are those set out in prescribed Form 1 (see Sch 1 to the Registration of Births and Deaths (Amendment) (England and Wales) Regulations 2009, and weblink in Appendix 1).

It is the duty:

(a)   of the father and mother of the child, and

(b)   in the case of the death or the inability of the father and mother, of each other qualified informant,

to give to the registrar, within 42 days of the birth of the child, information of the particulars required in the prescribed form concerning the birth of the child as at the date of the child's birth and, in the presence of the registrar, to sign the register (s 2 of the 1953 Act).

Where the parents are not married at the time of the child's birth the duty to register the child's birth is the mother's alone.

An unmarried father does not have any authority or duty to register a child's name. However, if the father who is not married to the mother at the time of the child's birth is named in the register of birth or on re-registration of the birth under the 1953 Act, then as a result of any such registration on or after 1 December 2003 he acquires parental responsibility for the child (s 111 of the Adoption and Children Act 2002), but he cannot register his name as the father without the consent of the mother. He has no right to choose the name of the child nor can he prevent the mother of the child from choosing a name of her choice (see further 2.5).

In the case of a child born to same sex female couples, who have entered into a civil partnership (and male civil partnership see 2.1.2) the woman who carried the child will be the child's mother and the other party to the relationship will be the parent provided the conditions set out in the Human Fertilisation and Embryology Act 2008 (HFEA 2008) are met (and male civil partnership see 2.1.2) and the references in ss 1 and 2(a) of the 1953 Act to the father of the child are to be read as a reference to the woman who is a parent (the 1953 Act as amended by the Sch 6, paras 2 and 3 to the HFEA 2008). Where, however, the same sex female couple have not entered into a civil partnership, the other woman, who is a party to the same sex relationship, is not required to give the information concerning the birth of the child, and the registrar cannot enter in the register the name of any woman as a parent of the child except as provided for in s 10 of the 1953 Act as amended by Sch 6, para 5(3) to the HFEA 2008 (see further 2.4)

Regulation 9(3)(b) provides that the surname to be entered on the register should be the surname by which, at the date of the registration of the birth, it is intended that the child shall be known.

Where a new born baby is found abandoned and no information as to the place of birth is available, the child's place of birth must be registered as the registration district and the sub-district where the child is found, or in any other case, where the child was abandoned. In such cases, the duty of giving the information and of signing the register is placed on the person who found the child, and on any person in whose charge the child may be placed. The entry for the child's date of birth will be the date which on the evidence produced appears to the Registrar to be the most likely date of birth of the child.

A superintendent registrar has the authority to register the birth of a child within 12 months of its birth (reg 11 of the 1987 Regulations).

Once the name of the child is registered, the registered name stands indefinitely. The name given in the Birth Register cannot be altered (see *Re H (Child's Name: First Name)* [2002] EWCA Civ 190, [2002] 1 FLR 973).

2.1.1 Who is the father, mother and who are the parents of a child?

At common law it is presumed that a child born to a married woman during the subsistence of the marriage is the child of her husband, that they both have parental responsibility for the child and have the power and duty to register the child's name and surname (see *Re W (A Child) (Change of Name), Re A (A Child) (Change of Name, Re B (Children) (Change of Name)* [1999] 2 FLR 930 and *Dawson v Wearmouth* [1999] 1 FLR 1167 at 1173).

Where the child is born to a woman after the marriage has been dissolved but within the period of gestation after the dissolution of the marriage, it is presumed that the former husband is the child's father (see *Re Overbury (Deceased)* [1954] 3 All ER 308). These presumptions are rebuttable by evidence.

2.1.2 Assisted reproduction

The issue of parenthood becomes more problematic in cases involving assisted reproduction and where persons are in a same sex relationship and have a child as a result of artificial insemination or as a result of entering into a surrogacy arrangement with a surrogate mother.

Married couple

Where a child was born to a married woman during the period between 4 April 1988 and 1 August 1991 as a result of artificial insemination with the sperm of someone other than her husband, the husband was regarded as the father of the child provided he had consented to the artificial insemination (s 27(1) of the Family Law Reform Act 1987).

A child born to a married woman after 1 August 1991 as a result of artificial insemination is treated as the child of the woman and her husband, and he will be treated as the child's father unless it is shown that he did not consent to the placing in her of the embryo or the sperm and eggs or to her insemination (as the case may be) (s 28(2) of the Human Fertilisation and Embryology Act 1990 (HFEA 1990)).

This remains the position under the HFEA 2008. Under the HFEA 2008, a woman who is carrying or has carried a child as a result of the placing in her of an embryo or of sperm and eggs and no other is treated as the mother of the child (s 33(1) of the HFEA 2008) irrespective of whether the woman was in the United Kingdom or elsewhere at the time of the placing in her of the embryo or the sperm and eggs (s 33(3) of the HFEA 2008).

If at the time of the placing in her of the embryo or of the sperm and eggs or of her artificial insemination the woman is married and the creation of the embryo carried by her was not brought about with the sperm of her husband, the husband and no other person will be treated as the father of the child unless it is shown that he did not consent to the placing in her of the embryo or the sperm and the eggs or to her artificial insemination as the case may be (s 35 of the HFEA 2008). They will both have parental responsibility for the child.

Where a child is born following treatment services provided to the mother without her husband's consent, the child is treated in law as having no father.

Posthumous use of sperm/embryo

By virtue of the Human Fertilisation and Embryology (Deceased Fathers) Act 2003 (which came into force on 1 December 2003 and amended the HFEA 1990), if the deceased donor was married to the mother or they were receiving treatment services together and his consent was not withdrawn to the use of his sperm after his death or the placing in the woman after his death of the embryo which was brought about using his sperm before his death, he will be treated as the father of the child provided that the woman elects in writing within 42 days of the child's birth for the deceased to be treated as the father of the child. The deceased man may be registered as the child's father on the child's birth certificate (s 28(5A) of the HFEA 1990 as amended).

Where the creation of the embryo was not brought about with the sperm of her husband and the husband died before the placing of the embryo in the wife, the deceased husband will be treated as the child's father provided that:

(a)   the husband had consented in writing and had not withdrawn his consent to the placing of the embryo in the woman after his death; and

(b)   to being treated as the father of the resulting child; and

(c)   the wife elects in writing within 42 days of the birth of the child for her husband to be treated a the father of the child; and

(d)   no other person is treated as the father pursuant to any other provision of the Act (s 28 (5C) of the HFEA 1990).

The provision relating to a married woman receiving treatment posthumously will after 1 October 2009 be considered under the HFEA 2008, which replaces the above provisions of the HFEA 1990. Section 39 provides that where a woman has a child as a result of sperm or embryo being placed in her or by artificial insemination and the creation of the embryo carried by her was brought about by using the sperm of a man after his death, or the creation of the embryo was brought about using the sperm of a man *before* his death but the embryo was transferred after the death of the man providing the sperm, the man will be treated as the father of the child provided that:

(a)   he had consented in writing to the use of his sperm after his death or to the placing in the woman after his death of the embryo which was brought about using his sperm before his death; and

(b)   he had consented to being treated as the father of any resulting child;

(c)   he had not withdrawn his consent (s 39(1)(c));

(d)   the woman elects in writing within 42 days (21 in Scotland) of the birth of the child for the man to be treated as the father of the child (s 39(d));

(e)   the woman is not a party to a civil partnership.

The deceased man may be registered as the child's father in the register of births (s 39(3)).

Where the deceased husband's sperm was not used he will be treated as the child's father provided all the conditions referred to above are satisfied (s 40(1)). He may be registered as the child's father in any register of birth.

Surrogacy

Pursuant to s 30 of the HFEA 1990, where a married heterosexual couple make an arrangement with a surrogate mother to carry a child for them using both the husband's sperm and the wife's egg fertilised in vitro (full surrogacy) or where the surrogate mother's egg is inseminated with the husband's sperm (partial surrogacy) with the intention that the surrogate mother should hand over the child at birth to the couple, the surrogate mother will be treated as the child's mother and the husband as the father. Provided he is registered in the birth register as the child's father he will have parental responsibility for the child. In order to extinguish the surrogate mother's right of parental responsibility, the father and his partner would need to apply for a parental order within 6 months of the child's birth. On the making of the order the parenthood of the child is transferred to the couple, with the effect that the child is treated in law as a child of the couple – the wife is treated as the child's mother and the husband the father – and they both have parental responsibility for the child.

Section 30 will be replaced by s 54 of the HFEA 2008 when it comes into force (expected April 2010).

Unmarried heterosexual couple

Where a woman and man, who are not married to each other seek licensed treatment services together in the United Kingdom, as provided for in the HFEA 1990, and as a result of the treatment a child is born to the woman, the woman's partner will be treated as the father (ss 28(3) and 29(1) of the HFEA 1990, and see *U v V (Attorney General Intervening)* [1997] 2 FLR 282 and *B and D v R (By Her Legal Guardian)* [2002] 2 FLR 843). However, he will not have parental responsibility for the child unless he is registered as the child's father on the birth certificate.

Where the fertility treatment is sought involving donor sperm and the couple separate after the creation of the embryos but before a successful implantation of the embryos, the man will not be treated as the legal father of the resulting child (see *Re R (IVF: Paternity of Child)* [2005] 2 FLR 843 HL).

Where due to an error, the sperm of a man, other than the woman's partner, is used, he cannot be treated as the father of the resulting child under s 28(2) of the HFEA 1990 because he had not consented to the actual treatment given to the woman. His consent involved her eggs being mixed with his sperm and not that of a donor (see *Leeds Teaching Hospital NHS Trust v A* [2003] 1 FLR 1091).

As from 1 October 2009 when Pt II of the HFEA 2008 came into force, in the case of a heterosexual couple, who are not married to each other, provided the woman does not have a female partner the conditions set out in ss 36 and 37 must be satisfied for the man to be treated as the child's father if his sperm was not used. The conditions are that:

(a)   the treatment must be provided in the United Kingdom by a licensed person; and

(b)   the man who seeks to be the father must be alive at that time;

(c)   the sperm is not that of the woman's male partner;

(d)   the man should have given the person responsible notice stating that he consents to being treated as the father of any child resulting from the treatment provided to the woman;

(e)   the woman too should have given notice stating that she consents to the man being so treated;

(f)   neither party has given notice to the person providing the treatment of the withdrawal of their respective consents;

(g)   the woman has not given a further subsequent notice that she consents to another man being treated as the father of the resulting child or a woman being treated as the parent of the resulting child; and

(h)   the couple are not within the prohibited degree of relationship (ss 36 and 37 of the HFEA 2008).

The notice of consent or withdrawal of consent must be in writing and must be signed by the person giving the notice (s 37(2) of the HFEA 2008). The notice must be given to the 'person responsible' (see page 13).

Posthumous use of sperm/embryo

Where the creation of the embryo carried by the woman was brought about by using the sperm of a man after his death, or the creation of the embryo was brought about before his death but the transfer of the embryo occurs after the death of the man, and the woman was not married to the man immediately before his death, but treatment services were being provided for them together before his death, he will be treated as the father of the child provided that:

(a)   he had consented in writing and had not withdrawn his consent, to the use of his sperm after his death or to the placing in the woman *after* his death of the embryo which was brought about using his sperm *before* his death; and

(b)   he had consented to being treated as the father of any resulting child; and

(c)   the woman elects in writing within 42 days of the child's birth for the man to be treated as the child's father (s 28(5B) of the HFEA 1990).

Where the sperm of the woman's partner was not used then provided all the above conditions are satisfied he will be treated as the child's father for the purpose of registering his particulars as the child's father in any register of birth (s 28(5D) of the HFEA 1990).

These provisions of the HFEA 1990 have now been replaced by s 39 of the HFEA 2008, which provides that if the woman receiving treatment is not married to the man and she is not in a civil partnership at the time and the creation of the embryo carried by her was brought about by using the sperm of her male partner after his death, or the creation of the embryo was brought about using his sperm *before* his death but the embryo was placed in the woman *after* his death, the man will be treated as the father of the child for the purposes of registering his particulars as the father of the child in any register of births subject to the following conditions being satisfied:

(a)   he must have consented in writing to the use of his sperm after his death which brought about the creation of the embryo or to the placing in the woman after his death of the embryo which was brought about with his sperm before his death; and

(b)   he must not have withdrawn his consent; and

(c)   he must have consented to being treated as the father of the child for the purposes of registering the child's birth in a register of births; and

(d)   the woman elects in writing within 42 (21 in Scotland) days of the child's birth that he should be treated as the child's father; and

(e)   no one else is to be treated as the father of the child pursuant to any other provision of the Act; and

(f)   no one is treated as a parent of the child under the provisions which apply to a woman in a civil partnership or agreed female parenthood (ie under s 42 or s 43, see female civil partnership 2.1.2).

Where donated sperm was used in the course of treatment provided to the woman in the United Kingdom by a licensed person, her deceased partner will be treated as the father of the child provided that:

(a)   he consented in writing and did not withdraw the consent to the placing of the embryo in the woman after his death and to being treated as the father of the child for the purposes of registering his particulars as the father of the child in any register of births; and

(b)   immediately before his death the 'fatherhood conditions' (see below) set out in s 37 were met in relation to the treatment proposed to be provided to the woman in the United Kingdom by a licensed person; and

(c)   the woman elects in writing within 42 days of the birth of the child for the man to be treated as the father for the purposes of registering the child's birth; and no one else is treated as the father of the child pursuant to any other provisions in the Act or as a parent of the child under s 43 or s 43 (see point (f) above).

The 'fatherhood conditions' are:

(a)   the deceased must have given the responsible person notice stating that he consents to being treated as the father of the resulting child from the treatment provided to the woman;

(b)   the woman has also given notice to the responsible person that she consents to the man being so treated; and

(c)   neither party has given notice of withdrawal of his/her consent; and

(d)   the woman has not given any further subsequent notice stating that she consents to another man being the father or another woman being treated as a parent of any resulting child; and

(e)   the couple are not within the prohibited degrees of relationship in relation to each other (s 37).

The notice must be given in writing and signed by each party. If either or both of them is unable to sign due to illness, injury or physical disability it may be signed by another person, provided it is signed at the direction of the incapacitated person and in his/her presence and in the presence of at least one witness, who attests the signature (s 37(2) and (3)).

The Registrar of Births is not, however, permitted to enter in the register as the father the name of the deceased person, unless the mother requests the registrar to make such an entry and supports the requests by producing the consent in writing and her election and a certificate of a registered medical practitioner as to the medical facts concerned and such other documentary evidence (if any) as the registrar considers appropriate (Sch 6, para 6 of the HFEA 2008).

Surrogacy

When the provisions of s 54 of the HFEA 2008 in relation to surrogacy come into force (expected April 2010), unmarried couples will be on an equal footing as married couples in applying for a parental order in relation to a child born as a result of a surrogacy arrangement between them and the surrogate mother.

Female civil partnership

Where a woman is a party to a civil partnership at the time of the placing in her of the embryo or the sperm and eggs or of artificial insemination anywhere in the world, she will be treated as the mother of the child born to her and the other party to the civil partnership will be treated as a parent of the child unless it is shown that she did not consent to the placing in her partner of the embryo or the sperm and eggs or the artificial insemination.

Where the embryo was created when the woman was a party to a civil partnership and the other party dies before the embryo is placed in the woman, she will be treated as a parent of the resulting child provided that:

(a)   the other party to the civil partnership (the deceased partner) has consented (and has not withdrawn that consent) to the placing of the embryo in the woman after the death of the other party; and

(b)   has consented to being treated as the parent of the resulting child; and

(c)   the woman elects in writing within 42 days of the birth of the child for the other party to the civil partnership to be treated as a parent of the child.

Female partners not in civil partnership

Where the women concerned are in a relationship but have not entered into a civil partnership and one of them has a child as a result of donor insemination, the other female will be treated as a parent of the resulting child provided the embryo or the sperm and eggs were placed in the woman or the woman was artificially inseminated in the course of treatment provided in a United Kingdom licensed clinic and at that time the 'female parenthood' conditions were met in relation to the other woman and she remained alive at that time. The 'female parenthood' conditions are:

(a)   the partner of the woman who is to carry the child must have given to the responsible person notice that she consents to being treated as a parent of the resulting child;

(b)   the woman, who will carry the child must give to the person responsible notice stating that she agrees to her partner being so treated;

(c)   neither of them must have given to the responsible person notice of the withdrawal of consent;

(d)   the woman must not have given a subsequent notice stating that she consents to another woman or a man (as the cae may be) being treated a a parent or a father of any resulting child; and

(e)   the couple must not be within the prohibited degrees of relationship in relation to each other.

The 'responsible person' is the person at the clinic under whose supervision the licensed treatment will be undertaken. The consents must be provided in writing and signed by the parties. In the case of either of the them being incapacitated the provisions outlined at page 14 apply (s 44(3)).

Where a woman is treated as a parent of the child under ss 42 and 43, no man can be treated as the father of the child (s 45).

Posthumous use of sperm/embryo

Similar provisions as those which apply to married couples under s 40 of the HFEA 2008 are provided in s 46 for the purposes of registering the deceased partner as a child's parent in the register of births where a civil partnership subsisted between the female partners. In the case where the female partners had not entered into a civil partnership, similar provisions as those which apply to unmarried couples are also provided for in s 46 so as to bring females in same sex relationships on the same footing as heterosexual married and unmarried couples.

The registration of the deceased person as a parent of the child in the register of births will not be made unless the conditions set out in Section 102A of the Births & Deaths Registration Act 1953 as amended by Sch 6, para 6 to the HFEA 2008 are complied with.

Male civil partnership

Male partners who have entered into a civil partnership may agree to use a surrogate to conceive and bear a child for them using their sperm. In this case the woman who gives birth to the child will be treated as the child's mother and the man who provided the sperm will be treated as the child's father. If the man is registered as the father of the child in the register of births he will have parental responsibility for the child. When the provisions of s 54 of the HFEA 2008 come into force (expected April 2010), male civil partners will be able to apply for a parental order and thus extinguish the mother's parental responsibility and acquire the rights of parenthood and joint parental responsibility. Currently however, if the couple wish to extinguish the mother's rights they must apply to adopt the child or apply for a residence order under s 8 of the Children Act 1989. (For other ways of acquiring parental responsibility see Chapter 3).

Late election by the mother

An election out of time may be made with the consent of the Registrar General. The application must be made to the Registrar General in writing setting out the reasons for the delay. His consent to such an application will only be granted if he is satisfied that there is a compelling reason for giving his consent to the making of such an election (s 52 of the HFEA 2008).

2.2 Re-registration or alteration of name

A child's name may be altered within 12 months of registration of its birth, but in this case the name must be re-registered. Section 13 of the 1953 Act applies where, before the expiry of 12 months from the date of the registration of the birth of any child, the name by which the child was registered is altered; or, if the child was registered without a name, and a name is later given to the child. In either case the registrar or superintendent registrar having the custody of the register in which the birth was registered should make an entry in the register upon delivery of a certificate in the prescribed form. In the case of a child who has a parent by virtue of s 42 or s 43 of the HFEA 2008 (see 2.1.2), the reference to the father of the child is to be treated as a regerence to the woman who is a parent of the child by virtue of that section (the 1953 Act as amended by Sch 6, para 8 to the HFEA 2008).

Regulation 14(1) of the 1987 Regulations prescribes two forms of certificate, namely:

(a)   where the name has been altered or given in baptism, the certificate must be in Form 3 (see weblink in Appendix 1);

(b)   where the name has been altered or given otherwise than in baptism, the certificate must be in Form 4 (see weblink in Appendix 1).

If the name was altered or given in baptism, the certificate in Form 3 must be signed either by the officiating minister or by the person having custody of the baptismal register. If the name was not given to the child in baptism, Form 4 is the appropriate form and must be signed by the 'father, mother, parent or guardian of the child or other person procuring the name of the child to be altered or given': s 13(1) (b) of the 1953 Act as amended by the HFEA 2008.

Upon delivery to him of an appropriate certificate, the registrar or superintendent registrar having custody of the register in which the birth is entered must enter the new name or altered name, without any erasure, in the register (s 13(1)). The registrar or superintendent registrar must enter, in space 17 of the entry, the name shown in the certificate, followed by the surname recorded in space 2 of the entry, and:

(a)   if the entry is made on production of a certificate in Form 3 that the name was given in baptism he must insert the words 'by baptism' and insert the date on which the child was baptised;

(b)   if the entry is made on production of a certificate in Form 4 he must add the words 'on certificate of naming dated the ...', and insert the date on which the certificate was signed (reg 14 of the 1987 Regulations).

The time limit within which the above procedure may be adopted is 12 months from the date of registration of birth. It is not possible to use this procedure for re-registration where the name is given or altered after the expiry of 12 months from the date on which the birth was first registered. In such cases the only course would be to make a statutory declaration to the effect that the birth certificate, and the baptismal certificate if the child has been baptised, relate to the same child.

Where a child's birth has not been registered and more than 12 months have elapsed from the date of its birth, the registrar or superintendent registrar must make a report to the Registrar General, stating to the best of his knowledge and belief:

(a)   the particulars required to be registered concerning the birth;

(b)   the source of the information; and

(c)   the name, surname and address of any qualified informant available to give information for the registration.

Once the Registrar General gives his written authority for the registration of the birth, the qualified informant will be required to make and sign the appropriate declaration in the presence of the registrar or the superintendent registrar (see reg 12 of the 1987 Regulations).

This provision applies both to an unmarried father of the child and to the woman who is a parent of the child by virtue of s 42 or s 43 of the HFEA 2008 (see pages 9-14).

2.3 Change to correct error in registration

Section 29(1) of the 1953 Act provides that no alteration shall be made in any register of live births, still births or deaths except as authorised by that Act or by any other Act.

Section 29(2) makes provision for clerical errors to be corrected, by any person authorised in that behalf by the Registrar General, in the prescribed manner and subject to the prescribed conditions.

An error of fact or substance in a register may be corrected by entry in the margin (without any alteration of the original entry) by the officer having custody of the register, upon production to him of a statutory declaration. The statutory declaration must set out the nature of the error and the true facts of the case. It must be made and delivered to the officer by two qualified informants of the birth with reference to which the error has been made, or in default of two qualified informants, then by two credible persons having knowledge of the true facts of the case.

Pursuant to the amendments made to s 29A of the 1953 Act by the HFEA 2008, where a person is wrongly shown as the father of the person to whose birth the entry relates or, in the case of same sex female couples where a woman is wrongly registered as a parent of a child, the entry may be corrected.

Once registered, the child's name may not be altered under these provisions unless there has been a genuine error. In *D v B (Surname: Birth Registration) sub nom D v B (Otherwise D) (Surname: Birth Registration)* [1979] Fam 38, the mother and father were married and living together when the child was conceived, but, before the child's birth, the mother left the father to live with another man. She assumed her partner's surname by deed poll. When the child was born she registered the child with the surname of her partner and not that of the natural father of the child. The father applied to the court for an order that the child should be known by his surname and that the mother should apply to alter the entry in the register of births to ensure that the child bore his surname. On appeal, it was held that since the surname entered by the mother in the register was the surname by which, at the date of the registration, it was intended the child should be known within the regulations then in force, and since it was not necessary that both parents should intend that the child should be known by that surname for there to be the requisite intention, there was no error in the entry within s 29(3) of the 1953 Act.

The 1953 Act does not require *both* parents to register the birth of a child. Either parent may do so, and give particulars of the name and surname by which it is intended the child is to be known. But to avoid problems it is advisable that both parents take an active part in the registration of their child's birth.

2.4 Registration of birth where parents not married or of a second female parent where parents are not civil partners

By virtue of the provisions of s 10 of the 1953 Act, as amended by s 24 of the Family Law Reform Act 1987 and s 108(4) of and Sch 12, para 6(1) and (2) to the Children Act 1989, where the parents are not married to each other at the time of the child's birth, the father has no power or duty to give information concerning the birth of the child. He has no right to intervene in the registration process and cannot prevent the mother registering the child with a surname of her choosing. As in the case of a father married to the mother, an unmarried father's only option is to apply under s 8 of the Children Act 1989 for a specific issue order seeking to change the name given to the child (see 3.6).

Sections 10 and 10A of the 1953 Act, as amended, set out the procedure to be followed where the parents are not married, and the evidence required before the name of any person may be registered as the father of a child when the birth is first registered.

Where the parents are not married, the registrar will not enter the name of any person as father of the child except:

(a)   at the joint request of the mother and the person stating himself to be the father of the child (in which case that person must sign the register together with the mother); or

(b)   at the request of the mother on production of:

     (i)   a declaration in the prescribed form (Form 2, see weblink in Appendix 1) made by the mother stating that that person is the father of the child; and

     (ii)   a statutory declaration made by that person stating himself to be the father of the child; or

(c)   at the request of that person on production of:

     (i)   a declaration in the prescribed form (Form 2, see weblink in Appendix 1) by that person stating himself to be the father of the child;

     (ii)   a statutory declaration made by the mother stating that that person is the father of the child;

(d)   at the request of the mother or that person (which shall in either case be in writing) on production of:

     (i)   a copy of any agreement made between them under s 4(1)(b) of the Children Act 1989 in relation to the child (ie a parental responsibility agreement); and

     (ii)   a declaration in the prescribed form (Form 6A) by the person making the request stating that the agreement was made in compliance with s 4 of the Children Act 1989 and has not been brought to an end by an order of a court; or

(e)   at the request of the mother or that person on production of:

     (i)   a certified copy of an order under s 4 of the Children Act 1989 giving that person parental responsibility for the child (ie a parental responsibility order); and

(ii) a declaration in the prescribed form (Form 6A) by the person making the request that the order has not been brought to an end by an order of a court; or

(f) at the request of the mother or that person on production of:

(i) a certified copy of an order under Sch 1, para 1 to the Children Act 1989 which requires that person to make any financial provision for the child and which is not an order falling within Sch 1, para 4(3); and

(ii) a declaration in the prescribed form (Form 6A) by the person making the request stating that the order has not been discharged by an order of a court; or

(g) at the request of the mother or that person on production of:

(i) a certified copy of any orders which are mentioned in s 10(1A) which has been made in relation to the child; and

(ii) a declaration in the prescribed form by the person making the request stating that the order has not been brought to an end or discharged by an order of a court.

The prescribed form for the purposes of points (d) to (g) above is Form 6A (see weblink in Appendix 1). Similar provisions apply in relation to registration and keeping of records of births occurring outside the United Kingdom among members of Her Majesty's armed forces, associated civilians and their respective families (see the Service Departments Registers Order 1959 (SI 1959/406 as amended by the Service Departments Registers (Amendment) Order 2009 (SI 2009/1736).

Point (d) above has been substituted as from 1 October 2003 by s 139(1) of and Sch 3, para 6 to the Adoption and Children Act 2002 to provide that the registrar may register the name of the father of the child at the request of the mother or the father of the child, on production of 'any agreement made between them under s 4(1)(b) of the Children Act 1989 in relation to the child'.

The orders referred to in s 10(1A) in point (g) above are:

(a) an order under s 4 of the Family Law Reform Act 1987 that that person shall have all the parental rights and duties with respect to the child;

(b) an order that that person shall have custody and care and control or legal custody of the child, made under s 9 of the Guardianship of Minors Act 1971 at a time when such an order could only be made in favour of a parent;

(c)   an order under s 9 or s 11B of the Guardianship of Minors Act 1971 which requires that person to make financial provision in relation to the child;

(d)   an order under s 4 of the Affiliation Proceedings Act 1957 naming that person as putative father of the child.

In the case of same sex female couples who have not entered into a civil partnership the HFEA 2008 inserts (as from a day to be appointed, see s 68(2)) into s 10 of the 1953 Act a further subsection which provides that no woman shall as a parent of the child by virtue of s 43 of the HFEA 2008 be required to give information concerning the birth of the child and the registrar must not enter the name of any woman as a parent of the child except where:

(a)   a joint request is made by the mother and the person stating herself to be the other parent of the child (in which case that person must sign the register together with the mother); or

(b)   a request is made by the mother together with a declaration in the prescribed form made by the mother stating that the other person to be registered ('the woman concerned'), is a parent of the child by virtue of s 43 of the HFEA 2008 and the woman concerned provides a statutory declaration confirming that she is the child's parent by virtue of s 43 of the HFEA 2008; or

(c)   a request is made by the woman concerned with a declaration by her in the prescribed form stating that she is a parent of the child by virtue of s 43 of the HFEA 2008 and a statutory declaration is made by the mother that the woman concerned is a parent of the child by virtue of s 43 of the HFEA 2008; or

(d)   a request is made by the mother or the woman concerned with of a copy of any parental responsibility agreement made between them under s 4ZA of the Children Act 1989 in relation to the child and a declaration in the prescribed form (Form 6A) by the person making the request that the agreement was made in compliance with the provision of s 4ZA of the Children Act 1989 and has not been brought to an end by an order of a court; or

(e)   the mother or the woman concerned makes a request and produces a certified copy of an order under s 4ZA of the Children Act 1989 giving the woman concerned parental responsibility for the child and a declaration in the prescribed form (Form 6A) by the person making the request stating that the order has not been brought to an end by an order of a court; or

(f) a request is made by the mother or the woman concerned with a certified copy of an order under Sch 1 to the Children Act 1989 which requires the woman concerned to make financial provision for the child and a declaration in the prescribed form (Form 6A) by the person making the request that the order has not been discharged by an order of a court.

Where a request is made by the other woman in accordance with the above conditions she must be treated as a qualified informant concerning the birth of the child and the such information and the signing of the register by her in the presence of the registrar acts as a discharge of any duty placed on any other qualified informant under s 2 of the 1953 Act.

2.5 Re-registration of birth where parents neither married nor civil partners

Section 10A of the 1953 Act, as amended by s 25 of the Family Law Reform Act 1987, the Children Act 1989 and the Adoption and Children Act 2002, provides for the father's name to be recorded in cases where the birth of a child, whose father and mother were not married to each other at the time of the birth, was registered but no person has been registered as the father of the child. The re-registration will be effected:

(a) at the joint request of the mother and the father; or

(b) at the request of the mother on production of:

    (i) a declaration in the prescribed form (Form 2) (weblink in Appendix 1) made by the mother stating that that person is the father of the child; and

    (ii) a statutory declaration made by that person stating himself to be the father of the child; or

(c) at the request of the father on production of:

    (i) a declaration in the prescribed form (Form 2) (see weblink in Appendix 1) by that person stating himself to be the father of the child; and

    (ii) a statutory declaration made by the mother stating that that person is the father of the child; or

(d) at the request of the mother or the father on production of:

    (i) 'any agreement made between them under section 4(1)(b) of the Children Act 1989'; and

    (ii) a declaration in the prescribed form (Form 6B, see weblink in Appendix 1 for a specimen form) by the person making the request stating that the agreement was made in compliance with s 4 of the Children Act 1989 and has not been brought to an end by an order of a court; or

(e)   at the request of the mother or that person on production of:

(i)   a certified copy of an order under s 4 of the Children Act 1989 giving that person parental responsibility for the child; and

(ii)   a declaration in the prescribed form (Form 6B) by the person making the request that the order has not been brought to an end by an order of a court; or

(f)   at the request of the mother or that person on production of:

(i)   a certified copy of an order under Sch 1, para 1 to the Children Act 1989 which requires that person to make any financial provision for the child and which is not an order falling within Sch 1, para 4(3); and

(ii)   a declaration in the prescribed form (Form 6B) by the person making the request stating that:

(ff)   in the case of a man who is treated as the father of the child by virtue of s 28(5A), (5B), (5C) or (5D) of the HFEA 1990, if the condition in s 10ZA(2) of the 1953 Act is satisfied (to be replaced by the provisions of HFEA 2008); or

(g)   at the request of the mother or that person on production of:

(i)   a certified copy of any orders which are mentioned in s 10A(1A) of the Children Act 1989 which has been made in relation to the child; and

(ii)   a declaration in the prescribed form by the person making the request stating that the order has not been brought to an end or discharged by an order of a court.

(h)   where the parents are in a female same sex relationship a request that the details of the partner of the mother of the child to be inserted as the parent of a child by virtue of s 42 or s 43 of the HFEA 2008. The woman who is classed as the parent of the child may be treated in the same way as a father of a child (see pages 12 and 13).

For the orders referred to in s 10A(1A) in point (g) above, see weblink in Appendix 1. The appropriate form under points (d) to (g) above is Form 6B.

Where a person stating himself to be the father of the child makes a request as set out above, to a registrar of births, he is regarded as a qualified informant concerning the birth of the child; and the giving of information by that person and the signing of the register by him in the presence of the registrar discharges any duty on any other qualified informant to register the birth (s 10A(2)).

The register is signed by the registrar. If the request is made by the mother alone she signs the register. Similarly, if the request is made by the father he signs the register. If the request is made jointly both parents sign.

With regard to same sex female couples, the HFEA 2008 inserts a new subs (1B) as from the day to be appointed which provides that where the parents are not civil partners and no person has been registered as a parent of the child by virtue of s 42, s 43 or s 46(1) or (2) of the HFEA 2008 (or as the father of the child) the re-registration can only be effected to show the woman concerned (ie the woman who is not the mother of the child) as a parent of the child by virtue of s 43 or s 46(1) or (2) of the HFEA 2008 (see pages 12 to 14):

(a)   at the joint request of the mother and the woman concerned; or

(b)   at the request of the mother on production of a declaration in the prescribed form made by the mother stating that the woman concerned is a parent of the child by virtue of s 43 of the HFEA 2008 and a statutory declaration made by the woman concerned stating herself to be a parent of the child by virtue of s 43 of the HFEA 2008; or

(c)   at the request of the woman concerned on production of a declaration in the prescribed form made by the woman concerned stating herself to be a parent of the child by virtue of s 43 of the HFEA 2008 and a statutory declaration by the mother stating that the woman concerned is a parent of the child by virtue of s 43 of the HFEA 2008; or

(d)   at the request of the mother or the woman concerned on production of a copy of a parental responsibility agreement made between them under s 4ZA(1)(b) of the Children Act 1989 in relation to the child and a declaration in the prescribed form by the person making the request stating that the agreement was made in compliance with s 4ZA of the Children Act 1989 and has not been brought to an end by an order of a court; or

(e)   at the request of the mother or the woman concerned on production of a certified copy of an order under s 4ZA of the Children Act 1989 giving the woman concerned parental responsibility for the child and a declaration in the prescribed form by the person making the request stating that the order has not been brought to an end by an order of a court; or

(f)   at the request of the mother or the woman concerned on production of a certified copy of an order under Sch 1, para 1 to the Children Act 1989 which requires the woman concerned to make any financial provision for the child and which is not an order falling within Sch 1, para 4(3) and a declaration in the prescribed form by the person making the request stating that the order has not been discharged by an order of a court; or

(g)   in the case of a woman who is treated as a parent of the child by virtue of s 46(1) or (2) of the HFEA 2008 (where the embryo is transferred after the death of the civil partner or intended female partner), provided the mother requests the registrar to make such an entry in the register and produces the relevant documents or in the case of the death or inability of the mother, the relevant documents are produced by some person who is a qualified informant.

The relevant documents are the consent in writing and election of the mother and a certificate of a registered medical practitioner as to the medical facts concerned and such other documents if any, as the registrar considers appropriate.

In each of the above instances the mother, the woman concerned and where applicable the informant, must sign the register.

Provision is also made under the HFEA 2008 for a female parent pursuant to s 43 to be registered or re-registered as the parent of a child if the child's parents subsequently enter into a civil partnership

2.6 Re-registration of births of legitimated persons

Section 2 of the Legitimacy Act 1976 provides that where the parents of an illegitimate child marry one another, the marriage shall, if the father of the illegitimate person is at the date of the marriage domiciled in England and Wales, render that child, if living, legitimate from the date of the marriage.

The 1953 Act, as amended by Sch 1, para 6 to the Legitimacy Act 1976 permits the re-registration of the births of persons recognised by English law as having been legitimated by the subsequent marriage of their parents.

As from 1 October 2009 when the relevant provisions of the HFEA 2008 came into force, similar provisions apply to cases of assisted reproduction where the parties are in a heterosexual relationship and subsequently marry each other or where they are in same sex relationship and later enter into a civil partnership, Sch 6, para 16 to the HFEA 2008 amends s 2 of the Legitimacy Act 1976 by inserting a new s 2A which provides that subject to the provision of the 1976 Act, where:

a person ('the child') has a parent ('the female parent') by virtue of Section 43 of the HFEA 2008 (treatment provided to a woman who agrees that the second woman to be parent),

(a)   at the time of the child's birth, the female parent and the child's mother are not civil partners of each other,

(b)   the female parent and the child's mother subsequently enter into a civil partnership, and

(c)   the female partner is at the date of the formation of the civil partnership domiciled in England and Wales,

(d)   the civil partnership shall render the child, if living, legitimate from the date of the formation of the civil partnership.

The parents will be able to re-register the birth of the legitimated person to show that he/she is the child of a person who is the parent of the child pursuant to s 43 of the HFEA 2008.

Section 9(1) of the Legitimacy Act 1976 places a duty on the parents of a legitimated person, or in cases where re-registration can be effected on information furnished by one parent and one of the parents is dead, on the surviving parent, to furnish to the Registrar General information, with a view to obtaining the re-registration of the birth of that person, within 3 months after the date of the marriage by virtue of which the person was legitimated. Section 56 of and Sch 6, Pt 1, para 18(b) to the HFEA 2008 extend this provision to female same sex couples on the formation of the civil partnership between them so that if they have had children together before entering into a civil partnership by assisted conception they can legitimise the children as from the date of the civil partnership.

By virtue of s 9(4) of the Legitimacy Act 1976, any parent who fails to give information as required by s 9 is liable, on summary conviction, to a fine.

The procedure for the re-registration of births of legitimated persons is set out in Pt V, regs 19 and 26 of the 1987 Regulations, as amended by the Registration of Births and Deaths (Amendment) Regulations 1994 and the Registration of Births and Deaths (Amendment) (England and Wales) Regulations 2009. These regulations make the following provisions relating to the re-registration of births in such cases:

Attendance and particulars on re-registration

19.   Where under section 14(1) of the Act the Registrar General authorises the re-registration of the birth of a legitimated person—

(a) except where Regulation 21 or 23 applies, and subject to section 14(2) of the Act (personal attendance as required by the Registrar General), the father and mother, or the other parent and mother of the legitimated person shall attend personally at the office of the relevant registrar for re-registration of the birth within such time as the Registrar General may direct;

(b) Regulation 7 (2) shall apply as to the particulars to be recorded in respect of the mother, father or other parent except that—

(i) in spaces 6 and 8 (b) of Form 1 (occupations), the occupations of the father and mother respectively need not be recorded as at both the date of birth and the date of entry,

(ii) in space 7 of Form 1, the surname to be recorded in respect of the mother of the child shall be her surname immediately after her marriage to the father or her civil partnership with the other parent, and

(iii) in space 9 (b) of Form 1, the surname (if any) to be entered shall be that in which the mother contracted her marriage or civil partnership to the father or other parent (respectively) of the child prior to re-registration.

Re-registration where mother, father, or other parent attends

20. – (1) Where the mother, father or other parent as the case may be, attend at the office of the relevant registrar to re-register a birth,, the registrar must—

(a) ascertain from them the particulars to be registered and enter them in spaces 1 to 13 of form 1 and;

(b) ask whoever is acting as the informant to verify the particulars and to sign the entry in space 14 of form 1;

(c) enter in space 15 of form 1 the date on which the entry is made and add the words 'On the authority of the Registrar General'; and

sign the entry in space 16 of form 1 and his official description.

Making of declaration where parent does not attend

21. – (1) Instead of attending personally at the office of the relevant registrar, a parent may with the written consent of the Registrar General verify the particulars required on re-registration in accordance with the following provisions of this Regulation.

(2) A parent who is in England or Wales may verify the particulars by making and signing before any registrar other than the relevant registrar a declaration of the particulars on the approved form.

(3) Any such declaration shall be attested by the registrar before whom it is made and sent by him to the relevant registrar.

(4) A parent who is not in England and Wales may verify the particulars by making and signing before a relevant authority, and sending to the Registrar General, a declaration of the particulars on an approved form.

(5) In paragraph (4) the 'relevant authority' means—

(a) in the case of a parent who is in Scotland, Northern Ireland, the Isle of Man, the Channel Islands or any part of the Commonwealth outside the British Islands or who is in the Irish Republic, a notary public and any other person who, in the place where the declaration is made, is authorised to administer oaths;

(b) in the case of a parent to whom sub-paragraph (a) above does not apply (and who is outside England and Wales), one of Her Majesty's consular officers, a notary public and any other person who, in the place where the declaration is made, is authorised to administer oaths so however that a declaration made otherwise than before a consular officer shall be authenticated by such officer if the Registrar General so requires;

(c) in the case of a parent who is a member of Her Majesty's Forces and who is not in the United Kingdom, any officer who holds a rank not below that of Lieutenant-Commander, Major or Squadron-Leader.

(6) In this regulation parent means, father, mother or other parent.

Re-registration in pursuance of declaration

22. On receiving the Registrar General's authority to re-register a birth together with his consent as to verification and the declaration made for the purposes of Regulation 21, the relevant registrar shall—

(a) copy the particulars recorded in the spaces of the declaration into the corresponding spaces of Form 1;

(b) enter in space 12 of Form 1 the qualification of the informant as 'father' or 'mother' or other parent, as the case may be;

(c) enter in space 14 of Form 1 the name of the declarant in the form in which he signed the declaration and add the words 'by declaration dated ...', inserting the date on which the declaration was made and signed;

(d) complete the entry as provided in regulation 20(3)(c) and (d).

Re-registration where particulars not verified by parent

23. Where, in a case to which any of the provisos to section 14(1) of the Act applies, the Registrar General authorises the relevant registrar to re-register the birth of a legitimated person notwithstanding that the particulars to be registered have not been verified by (ie mother father or other parent) either parent, the registrar shall—

(a) copy the particulars recorded in the spaces of the authority into the corresponding spaces of Form 1;

(b) enter in space 14 the words 'On the authority of the Registrar General' without any further entry in that space;

(c) enter in space 15 the date on which the entry is made and sign the entry in space 16, adding his official description.

Noting of previous entry

24. Where the birth of a legitimated person is re-registered in accordance with Regulation 20, 22 or 23 the superintendent registrar or registrar having custody of the register in which the birth was previously registered shall, when so directed by the Registrar General, note in the margin of the previous entry the words 'Re-registered under section 14 of the Births and Deaths Registration Act 1953, on ...', inserting the date of the re-registration.

Certified copies of re-registered entries

25. Where an application is made to a superintendent registrar or registrar for a certified copy of the entry of the birth of a legitimated person whose birth has been re-registered in a register in his custody—

(a) he shall supply a certified copy of the entry of re-registration;

(b) a certified copy of the superseded entry shall not be supplied except with the authority of the Registrar General.

Re-registration where person born at sea

26. – (1) Where under section 14(1) of the Act the Registrar General authorises the re-registration of the birth of a legitimated person who was born at sea and whose birth was included in a return sent to the Registrar General—

(a) the mother, father or other parent of the legitimated person shall verify the particulars required on re-registration by making and signing on an approved form a declaration of those particulars before a registrar or a relevant authority as defined in Regulation 21(5);

(b) the mother, father or other parent shall send the declaration to the Registrar General.

(2) In relation to any case to which this Regulation applies, section 14(1) of the Act shall apply with the modification that a person deputed for the purpose by the Registrar General shall on receiving the Registrar General's authority, together with the declaration made by the mother, father or other parent under paragraph (1), effect re-registration by—

(a) making the entry in a register to be kept at the General Register Office in Form 7, copying the particulars recorded in the spaces of the authority into the corresponding spaces of the form;

(b) noting in the margin of any previous record of the birth in the custody of the Registrar General the words 'Re-registered under section 14 of the Births and Deaths Registration Act 1953, on ...', inserting the date of re-registration; and

(c) sending a copy of the previous record, including a copy of the marginal note, certified under the seal of the General Register Office, to the authority from whom that record was received by the Register General.

2.7 Re-registration after declaration of parentage

By virtue of s 55A of the Family Law Act 1986, as amended, any person may make an application to the High Court, or a county court or a family proceedings court, for a declaration as to whether or not a person named in the application is or was the parent of another person named in the application. 'Parent' includes a person who is to be treated as a parent by virtue of the HFEA 2008 (see also *Re R (IVF: Paternity of Child)* [2003] 1 FLR 183).

Any person may also apply to the court for one (or for one or the other) of the following declarations:

(a)   a declaration that he has become a legitimated person;

(b)   a declaration that he has not become a legitimated person.

For the procedure for application for declarations of legitimacy, legitimation or parentage, see the procedural table at 2.8.1.

Where a declaration is made as to parentage the authorised officer of the court must notify the Registrar General of the making of that declaration; and, under the provisions of s 14A of the 1953 Act as amended, where the Registrar General receives a notification of the making of a declaration of parentage in respect of a person and it appears to him that the birth of that person should be re-registered, he must authorise the re-registration of that person's birth.

Re-registration under any of the above provisions will probably result in the change of the person's surname as recorded in the original registration.

2.8 Procedural tables

2.8.1 Declaration of legitimacy or legitimation

Who may apply?	Any person (usually the person who wishes to establish his/her status)	FLA 1986, s 56(1), (2); FPR 1991, r 3.14
Venue	High Court or county court	FLA 1986, ss 56(1), (2), 63; FPR 1991, r 3.14
Steps to be taken before issuing proceedings	All documents must be served on the Attorney General at least one month before the petition is filed	FPR 1991, r 3.16(4)
The application	By petition which must include the details set out in FPR 1991, r 3.14(1), App 2, para 4 and, where appropriate, r 3.16(2)	FPR 1991, rr 2.2(1), 3.14(1), 3.16(2), (12)
Fee payable	£300	FPFO 2008, fee 1.2
Documents to be filed with the petition	A copy of the applicant's birth certificate (unless otherwise directed)	FPR 1991, r 3.14(2)
	Affidavit verifying petition and identifying those affected	FPR 1991, r 3.16(1)
Respondents	The applicant's parents (if alive)	FPR 1991, r 3.14(3)
	The Attorney General has a right to intervene	FLA 1986, s 59(2); FPR 1991, r 3.16(7), (9), (10)

	Other parties may be joined	FPR 1991, rr 3, 16(6), (8)
Service of proceedings	In accordance with FPR 1991, rr 2.9, 9.3 and 10.6	FPR 1991, r 3.16(12)
Answer to petition	Within 28 days after service of the petition	FPR 1991, rr 2.12(1), 3.16(12), 10.8(2)(a)
Interlocutory hearings	For directions	FPR 1991, rr 3.16(12), 2.13–2.25
Final hearing		FPR 1991, rr 2.32–2.42, 3.16(12)
Order	A declaration that the applicant is the legitimate child of his parents; or that the applicant has/has not become legitimated	FLA 1986, 56(1), (2)
Form	M31	

Note: with regard to the registration of births in Wales, the prescribed forms are those set out in the Registration of Births and Deaths (Welsh Language) Regulations.

2.8.2 Declaration of parentage under the Family Law Act 1986

Who may apply?	A parent, the child or any other person with sufficient personal interest	FLA 1986, s 55A; FPR 1991, r 3.13
Which court?	High Court, county court magistrates' court	FLA 1986, s 55A; FPR 1991, r 3.13
Application	By petition containing unless otherwise directed, the details required by FPR 1991, r 3.13(1) App 2, para 4, and where appropriate r 3.16(2)	FPR 1991, rr 2.2(1), 3.13(1), 3.16(2), (12)

Fee	£300	FPFO 2008, fee 1.2
Documents to accompany petition	Copy of the birth certiicate of the person whose parentage is in issue	FPR 1991, r 3.13(2)
	Affidavit verifying petition identifying those affected	FPR 1991, r 3.16(1)
Respondents	Person whose parentage is in issue, anyone who is alleged to be the mother, father or parent of that person	FPR 1991, r 3.13(3)
Other parties	Attorney General may intervene	FLA 1986, s 59(2); FPR 1991, r 3.16(7)(9) and (10)
Service	In accordance with FPR 1991, rr 2.9, 9.3 and 10.6	FPR 1991, r 3.16(2)
Answer	28 days after service	FPR 1991, rr 2.12(1), 3.16(2), 10.8
Order	Declaration that person named in the petition is or was the parent of the applicant or another named person	FLA 1986, s 55A
Form	M30 in High Court and county court;	
	FL424 in family proceedings court	

Abbreviations used in the tables above:

FLA 1986: Family Law Act 1986;

FPR 1991: Family Proceedings Rules 1991 (SI 1991/1247);

FPFO 2008: Family Proceedings Fees Order (SI 2008/1054); Family Proceedings Fees (Amendment) Order (SI 2008/2856).

3 Changing a Child's Name

3.1 Introduction

A decision to change a child's name is one of great importance and ought not be taken unilaterally no matter what the circumstances may be. Where a parent considers that the circumstances are such that a change is in the best interest of the child, the appropriate course is to seek the other parent's consent and, if this is not forthcoming, to apply to the court for permission to make the change.

A child is not competent to change his or her name (*Re T (Otherwise H) (An Infant)* [1963] Ch 238). In *Re PC (Change of Surname) sub nom Re C (Minors) (Change of Surname); Re P (Change of Surname: Parent's Rights)* [1997] 2 FLR 730 at 733E, Holman J determined that:

(a)   where only one person has parental responsibility for a child he had the right and power lawfully to cause a change of surname without any other permission or consent;

(b)   where two or more persons have parental responsibility for a child, one of them could only lawfully effect a change of surname if everyone with parental responsibility consented in writing. By law a parent did not have the right, power or authority unilaterally to change a legitimate child's surname without the consent of the other parent.

(c)   where two or more persons have parental responsibility for a child and the child is the subject of a residence order or a care order, the child's name can only lawfully be changed if all those with parental responsibility consent in writing. In the absence of consent an order of the court is required (see ss 13(1) and 33(7) of the Children Act 1989).

Holman J also stated that it was inappropriate for children aged 12, 10 and 6 to sign a formal document, such as a deed of change of surname (see Chapter 4).

In the case of an older child, who is '*Gillick*' competent and in particular a child who is 16 years of age or over, the consent of the child may be required. Where the dispute between the parties cannot be resolved by agreement and an application has to be made to the court, an older child's wishes and feelings will be relevant to any decision the court makes (see *Re PC (Change of Surname) sub nom Re C (Minors) (Change of Surname); Re P (Change of Surname: Parent's Rights)* [1997] 2 FLR 730).

A child may acquire a name, particularly a surname not registered at birth, as his surname involuntarily. Because a child is assumed to have the same name as that of the parent with whom the child lives and upon whom the child is dependent, if that parent has changed his or her name, as in the case of a mother who remarries or cohabits with another, the likelihood is that in due course the child will involuntarily become known by the same surname as that of the parent. However, it cannot be stressed enough that a parent with whom the child lives is not permitted to take any steps, eg by registering the child at school or with a GP, which would result in the child's name being changed, without the consent of the other parent.

When considering changing a child's name it should be borne in mind that, in *Re PC (Change of Surname)sub nom Re C (Minors) (Change of Surname); Re P (Change of Surname: Parent's Rights)* [1997] 2 FLR 730, when referring to the responses of schools, doctors and other holders of official or formal records, it was stated:

> no responsible school, doctor, education or health authority or similar body could want unwittingly to aid or implement an unlawful act. Any change of surname is an important act in the life of a child, carrying with it emotional and psychological as well as social and practical consequences. It is hard to reverse. Any doubt about it needs to be resolved *before*, not after, any formal steps to implement the change have taken place.

In *Re C (A Minor) (Change of Surname)* [1998] 2 FLR 656, Ward LJ stated that at the first signs of a dispute about the child's name the disputed issues ought to be referred to the court: 'Whether that is simply a matter of wisdom, common decency, courtesy, or whatever, and not a binding obligation I leave to one side. But it is highly advisable that at the first signs of a dispute about the child's name the court should be involved'.

The House of Lords in *Dawson v Wearmouth* [1999] 2 AC 308 indicated that where there is a dispute over a child's surname the proper course is to bring the matter before the court for resolution. This is done by applying for a specific issue order under s 8 of the Children Act 1989, which means asking the court to give directions on the specific question which has arisen, or which may arise, in connection with any aspect of parental responsibility.

3.2 Parents married to each other or in a civil partnership and in agreement

Where the child's parents are married to each other they have joint parental responsibility for the child and, as with any other decision relating to the child's care and upbringing, if they are in agreement they jointly have the right to name their child and change the child's name. This right applies to both the child's forenames and surname. This can be achieved, as in the case of an adult, by assuming the use of the new name. Although not legally necessary, it is advisable, to avoid any problems or conflict, for the change to be evidenced by executing and enrolling a deed poll in accordance with the Enrolment of Deeds (Change of Name) Regulations 1994 (SI 1994/604) and *Practice Direction: Child: Change of Surname* [1995] 1 WLR 365 (see Chapter 4), or a statutory declaration or notarial instrument (see 5.3 and 5.4) (see *D v B (Surname: Birth Registration) sub nom D v B (Otherwise D) (Surname: Birth Registration)* [1979] Fam 38 and *R (BM) v R (DN)* [1977] 1 WLR 1256 at 1260G).

3.3 Children born out wedlock or to female partners not in a civil partnership

In the case of an unmarried couple, if the child was born before 1 December 2003 the child's father does not have parental responsibility for the child unless he acquires it by entering into a 'parental responsibility agreement' with the mother, granting the father parental responsibility for the child, or there is a court order granting him parental responsibility and/or a residence order. The father can also acquire parental responsibility by marrying the mother or by adopting his child, but until he takes some active step to acquire parental responsibility for his child the mother alone has parental responsibility and she can change the child's name without consulting the father (*Re PC (Change of Surname) sub nom Re C (Minors) (Change of Surname); Re P (Change of Surname: Parent's Rights)* [1997] 2 FLR 730 and *Re W (A Child) (Illegitimate Child: Change of Surname) sub nom Re W (A Child) (Change of Name); Re A (A Child) (Change of Name); Re B (Children) (Change of Name)* [1999] 2 FLR 930). The father in such a situation has a right to apply to the court for a specific issue order reversing a change. However, it was observed in *Dawson v Wearmouth* [1999] 2 AC 308 that the registration or change of a child's surname is a profound and not merely formal issue, whatever the age of the child. Any dispute on such an issue must be referred to the court for determination whether or not there is a residence order in force and whoever has or has not parental responsibility. No disputed registration or change should be made unilaterally.

The need to obtain the consent of the other parent or leave of the court before any change is made in the child's surname was also emphasised in *Re T (A Minor) (Change of Surname)* [1998] 2 FLR 620 and *Re C (A Minor) (Change of Surname)* [1998] 2 FLR 656.

In relation to a child born after 1 December 2003, s 111 of the Adoption and Children Act 2002 amends s 4 of the Children Act 1989 to provide that an unmarried father will acquire parental responsibility for his child if:

(a)   his name is registered or re-registered as the child's father under the provisions of ss 10 and 10A of the 1953 Act (see 2.4 and 2.5) or the equivalent statutory provisions applicable in Scotland and Northern Ireland;

(b)   he and the child's mother make a parental responsibility agreement providing for him to have parental responsibility for the child; or

(c)   the court, on the father's application, orders that he should have parental responsibility for the child (s 4 of the Children Act 1989).

It should be noted however, that an unmarried father will only be able to have his name placed on the birth certificate at the registration or re-registration of the child's birth under the relevant enactments if the mother agrees to his name being so registered. Once he acquires parental responsibility by being registered as the child's father he will continue to have parental responsibility until it is removed by an order of the court on an application made by a person with parental responsibility. He thus has a right to choose his child's name and his consent is necessary before any change in the child's name is made.

Where an unmarried father's name is not registered as the father on the register of births but he wishes to be so registered he may apply to the court either himself or jointly with the mother to have the birth re-registered (s 10A of the 1953 Act as amended by s 93(2) of the Children Act 1989). He can achieve this by making an application for a parental responsibility order or by applying for a declaration of parentage under s 55A of the Family Law Act 1986, provided he is able to demonstrate a genuine interest in such a declaration and that it is in the best interest of the child (for procedure see Chapter 2). In any event where a dispute arises relating to the child's name or change of name he may apply to the court under s 8 of the Children Act 1989 for a specific issue order.

A man who is not registered as the child's father may nevertheless acquire parental responsibility for his child by:

(a) marrying the mother and legitimising his child;

(b) entering into a parental responsibility agreement with the child's mother;

(c) by applying to the court under the Children Act 1989 that he should be granted parental responsibility;

(d) by obtaining a residence order under s 8 of the Children Act 1989;

(e) by adopting the child.

In relation to those couples who are in same sex relationship but who have not entered into a civil partnership the same principles apply. Even where the partner does not have parental responsibility he/she can apply under s 8 of the Children Act 1989 for the issue to be determined by the court. It should also be noted that when s 54 of the HFEA 2008 comes into force (expected April 2010), male couples in a relationship will be able to apply for a parental order in cases involving surrogacy (see further pages 12 & 14).

3.4 Step-parents

It is now also possible for a step-parent to acquire parental responsibility by either:

(a) entering into a parental responsibility agreement with the child's natural parents; or

(b) applying to the court for an order that the step-parent should have parental responsibility for the child (Children Act 1989, s 44).

However, even if the step-parent acquires parental responsibility in either of the two ways set out above, any change in the name of the step-child would need the agreement of both parents of the child and in the absence of consent an application should be made to the court for an order.

Where an agreement is reached without recourse to litigation, the agreement should be recorded in writing. Where the change is made by deed poll it will be necessary to provide written evidence of consent before the deed can be enrolled.

3.5 Parents separated: residence order in force

Section 13(1)(a) of the Children Act 1989 provides that where a residence order in respect of a child is in force, no person may cause the child to be known by a new surname without either the written consent of every person who has parental responsibility for the child, or the permission of the court. Section 33(7) provides that while a care order is in force with respect to a child, no person may cause the child to be known by a new surname without either the written consent of every person who has parental responsibility for the child or the leave of the court.

Thus a parent with a residence order in his or her favour cannot unilaterally change the child's name. If consent from the other parent cannot be obtained, then the parent who is desirous of changing the child's name must apply to the court for permission to do so. In the case of a parent who opposes the change, an application to the court should be made promptly for a specific issue order/prohibited steps order under s 8 of the Children Act 1989. Where appropriate a prohibited steps order without notice should be obtained or alternatively the court should be asked to abridge the time for service and to deal with the issue on short notice.

Where the court has granted leave, or the other parent has given consent to changing a child's surname, it may be desirable to effect the change by deed poll; if the deed poll is to be enrolled, the requirements of the Enrolment of Deeds (Change of Name) Regulations 1994 and *Practice Direction: Child: Change of Surname* [1995] 1 WLR 365 must be met (see Chapter 4, 4.3). It is not, however, essential to execute a deed poll, nor for a deed poll to be enrolled.

3.6 Disputes: private law applications

In deciding an application for a change of name, the court, as in all other disputes relating to children, has always had regard to the welfare and interests of the child as its paramount consideration. This was the principle applied in cases prior to and since the Guardianship of Minors Acts 1971 and 1973. Under the Children Act 1989, on any application, the child's welfare is the court's paramount consideration (s 1(1) of the Children Act 1989). The court is required to have regard to the matters set out in s 1(3) of the Act, the 'welfare checklist', in applying the welfare principle.

However, there seems to be a difference of opinion on the principles which the court should apply in cases involving a change of name if the application is brought under s 13(1) of the Children Act 1989 (for leave) as opposed to an application under s 8 of the Act (for a specific issue or prohibited steps order). Whilst it is accepted that in both cases the child's welfare is the paramount consideration, in some cases the court has approached an application issued under s 13(1) on the basis that the welfare checklist does not apply to a s 13 application. The ground for this approach seems to be on the assumption that because the FPR 1991 makes specific provision for an application under s 13 to be made in Form C44 and for an order under s 8 to be in Form C43, the welfare checklist does not strictly apply to an application under s 13(1) (see *Re B (Change of Surname)* [1996] 1 FLR 791). In *Re M, T, P, K and B (Care: Change of Name)* [2000] 2 FLR 645, it was held that whilst there is no mandatory requirement to apply the welfare checklist to a private law application for a name change brought under s 13 the difference between a s 13 application and one brought under s 8 was 'theoretical than real because the checklist factors would be considered in relation to a s 13 application as they would be in applications under ss 8 and 33(7).

It is submitted that the terms of s 13 merely seeks to prevent a parent who has a residence order in his/her favour acting unilaterally and does not seek to suggest that the criteria which the court applies when determining the conflict between the parties should be different. In any event, which ever route is followed the court will invariably have to consider the factors set out in the welfare check list when it determines the application for a change of name. It seems illogical that the basis of the court's decision in such cases should turn on the route adopted by the parties in dispute.

In cases where a parent becomes aware of an intention of a change of name of a child by the parent who has day-to-day care of the child or has a residence order in his/her favour, it is suggested that if there is opposition to the change, the parent who is opposed to the change should be advised to take the pro-active step of issuing an application under s 8 for a specific issue/prohibited steps order.

It should also be noted that whilst case law lays down guidelines, each case must be decided on its own facts and all relevant matters relating to that specific case must be considered (*Re W (A Child) (Illegitimate Child: Change of Surname) sub nom Re W (A Child) (Change of Name); Re A (A Child) (Change of Name); Re B (Children) (Change of Name)* [1999] 2 FLR 930, see also Robert George, 'Changing Names, Changing Places: Reconsidering s 13 of the Children Act 1989' [2008] Fam Law 1121).

The following cases illustrate the approach of the courts before and since the Children Act came into force.

In *Re T (Otherwise H) (An Infant)* [1963] Ch 238, on divorce, the mother had been granted custody of the child. She married and acquired her second husband's surname. Without any communication to the natural father the mother executed a deed poll purporting to change the child's surname to that of her second husband. When the father discovered the change he objected, and applied to the court for the deed poll to be cancelled, or for a deed poll to be registered which would revert the child's surname to that of his natural father. It was held that the mother of a child of tender years could not of her own motion change her name as such a change involved a conscious decision to do so. Further, Buckley J said ([1963] Ch 238 at 242):

> In the case of a divided family of this sort it is always one of the aims of the court to maintain the child's contact, respect and affection with and for both parents so far as the circumstances will permit. But to deprive the child of her father's surname, in my judgement, is something which is not in the interest of the child because, I think, it is injurious to the link between the father and the child to suggest to the child that there is some reason why it is desirable that she should be called by some name other than her father's name. The fact that there has been a divorce and that the father was the person against whom the decree was granted is an insufficient view. For these reasons, in my judgement, not only was the infant's mother incompetent to take a step on behalf of the infant which was of a kind calculated to have quite far-reaching effects upon the child but also, in my view it was a step which was not in the interest of the infant and which the court ought not to assist in any way.

In *Y v Y (Child: Surname)* [1973] Fam 147, on divorce, the custody of the two children of the family, both girls, was committed to the mother in 1964. In the following summer the mother stopped all contact between the father and the children. In January 1965 the mother re-married and in July 1965, without consulting the father, she registered the children on the school register by the surname of her second husband. When the father discovered the change in the surname he applied to the court for an order that the children should resume their former surname. When the matter came before the court the girls were aged 13 and 9. It was held that an order for custody did not entitle the mother unilaterally to change the children's surname; to do so would infringe the father's rights as natural guardian; nor was the father entitled unilaterally to cause a change of name. Where the court had become seized of matters which concern a child, a parent who wishes to take any important step affecting the child, such as a change of surname, should seek the decision of the court. In the particular circumstances of the case, whatever the decision might have been in 1965, the court had to decide the issue after a lapse of some

4 years in a way which was in the best interests of the children. To change the older girl's name so that it reverted to that of her natural father would cause her embarrassment, and although the same did not apply to the younger child, it was plain that both children should have the same surname. The court decided that it was best to let the children retain their step-father's name.

In *Re D (Minors) (Adoption by Parent)* [1973] Fam 209, although the case concerned an application for adoption by the mother and her second husband, one of the motives behind the application was to give the children the surname of the second husband. It was held that this could not be a legitimate reason for adoption, nor would it generally be in the interest of the children.

In *Re WG* (1976) 6 FL 210, after the parents of a little girl divorced, they both re-married and the father went to Singapore to work. He did not have contact with the child thereafter. When the child started school the mother was urged by the school to change the child's name to that of her second husband. At first instance, permission was given to the mother to retain the child's new name. However, on appeal it was held:

> Whilst [there was] no doubt that there was administrative convenience from the school's point of view in having the same surname as the people with whom [the child] was living, it was wrong to attach too much importance to considerations in connection with schooling as against the longer term interests of [the child]. It was, of course, important to bear in mind all the way through that it was the paramount interests of the child with which their Lordships were concerned. It had not been suggested on either side here that the court should approach the decision in the case from any other point of view. But his Lordship thought it important that it should be realised that the mere fact that there had been a divorce, that the mother had re-married and had custody of the child, and had a name different from that of the child, was not a sufficient reason for the changing of the surname. The court recognised the importance of maintaining a link with the father, unless he had ceased to have an interest in the child or there were some grounds – having regard to his character or behaviour – which made it undesirable for him to have access to the child at all. It must greatly tend to create difficulties in the relation between father and a child if the child ceased to bear the father's name – especially if, as here, the child had come to address her step-father as 'daddy' and refer to her father as 'old daddy'.

The appeal was allowed and the mother's application dismissed.

In *L v F* (1978) *The Times*, 1 August, where the mother had changed the children's name to that of their step-father, it was held that the issue of change of name affected the best interests and psychological welfare of the children. In the circumstances it would be beneficial to the children to maintain contact and relationship with their father. The mother's application was refused.

In *Crick v Crick* (1977) 7 Fam Law 239, the mother registered the children at school in their new name but had not taken any other formal steps to change the children's name. The children were aware of their true surname but were not concerned about the use of the new name. The court permitted the mother to continue using the new name.

In *D v B (Surname: Birth Registration) sub nom D v B (Otherwise D) (Surname: Birth Registration)* [1979] Fam 38, the mother had changed her surname by deed poll and on the birth of her child she had registered the child's name in her assumed name. The Official Solicitor, representing the child, recommended that in the circumstances it was not in the interest of the child to be called by his father's surname as this would cause the child embarrassment when he attended school and would cause him distress insofar as he would be the only one in the family with a different name. The mother's application to retain the child's name as registered was allowed.

In *W v A sub nom W v A (Child: Surname)* [1981] Fam 14, it was said (per Dunn LJ at 21):

> It is a matter for the discretion of the individual judge hearing the case, seeing the parents, possibly seeing the children, to decide whether or not it is in the interest of the child in the particular circumstances of the case that his surname should or should not be changed; and the judge will take into account all the circumstances of the case, including no doubt where appropriate, any embarrassment which may be caused to the child by not changing his name and on the other hand the long term interests of the child, the importance of maintaining the child's link with his paternal family and the probable stability or otherwise of the mother's re-marriage. I only mention those as typical examples of the kind of considerations which arise in these cases, but the judge will take into account all the relevant circumstances in the particular case.

In *R v R (Child: Surname)* (1982) 3 FLR 345, the mother was permitted to continue to allow the child to be known at school and to her friends in the mother's new surname because the situation had become irreversible and an order to that effect was regarded as in the best interest of the child.

In *Re F (Child: Surname)* [1993] 2 FLR 837, the parents of two children separated in 1992. The mother remarried in 1993. She intended that the children should have a new double-barrelled surname incorporating her maiden name and the surname of her second husband. The father objected. The eldest child had a surname which was different from that of her mother. Refusing the mother's application for permission to change the children's name, Ralph LJ said:

> Given the importance which the law requires us to attach to the changing of the child's name, I see nothing in the material before the judge which indicates that it is of any significance whatever for the future well-being of the children to change their name. The time over which they have been alone with their mother is short. There is no established pattern of them being known by the mother's maiden name and, indeed, there is no attempt by the father to prevent the use when convenient of another name of these little girls in circumstances in school.

In *G v A (Children: Surname)* [1995] 2 FCR 223, the children's surname was registered on their birth certificates as that of their natural father. The parties separated, and when the children were aged 4 and 6 they assumed the name of their mother's cohabitee whom she later married. The natural father was denied parental responsibility by the mother although he saw his children regularly. The father applied for a prohibited steps order preventing the mother changing the children's surname, and a specific issue order concerning the name the children were to use in future. He also applied for parental responsibility. The court prohibited the mother from effecting a change in the children's name, but since the children had been known by the surnames of both their natural father and their step-father, the court permitted the children to be known by the hyphenated surname of both fathers, without any change in their registered surname, on all official documents. The father was also granted parental responsibility. In deciding the issues the court had regard to the welfare of the children and, in so doing, to the fact that they had come to be known at school by the surname of their step-father, their father and by both surnames. In order to reduce confusion for the children, the court directed that the name be hyphenated.

In *Re B (Change of Surname)* [1996] 1 FLR 791, a couple had three children, the eldest of whom was an adopted child. The parents' marriage broke down in 1986 and by 1988 the mother had begun to live with another partner and she re-married in 1992. By 1990 contact between the children and the father had broken down by reason of the children's objections to it. Since the mother's re-marriage the children had become known by their step-father's surname, particularly at school. The mother applied for permission to change the children's surname. At the date of the hearing the children were aged 16, 14 and 12. They expressed their wish, through the court welfare officer, to be known by the new name, as their surname had been a source of embarrassment to them. The application was refused. The court held that whilst it was virtually unknown to family law, in relation to residence or contact, that an order should be made which ran flatly contrary to the wishes of children who were shown to be *Gillick* competent (within the test applied in *Gillick v West Norfolk and Wisbech Area Health Authority and Another* [1986] 1 AC 112), there was an important distinction to be drawn between the making of a residence or contact order and the current application. It was accepted as being of fundamental importance for every child to have an enduring relationship with both parents, notwithstanding their separation; to allow the application would have served further to weaken the link between the children and their father.

In *Re PC (Change of Surname) sub nom Re C (Minors) (Change of Surname), Re; P (Change of Surname: Parent's Rights)* [1997] 2 FLR 730, on the divorce of their parents, the three children, aged 12, 10 and 6, by agreement, continued to live with their mother and have contact with their father. The father ceased to have contact and the mother re-married and changed her surname. She stated that the children wished to be known by the surname of their step-father and drew up a deed poll for the new name, without the consent of the natural father. The school authorities refused to register the children under the new name. It was held that the school authorities were correct in refusing to change their records, as they were under an obligation to satisfy themselves that everyone who had parental responsibility had consented to the change of name. In the circumstances, however, the court permitted the children to continue to be known by their new name but directed that the mother should not take any steps to cause, encourage or permit any person or body to use the new surname without the prior consent of the father or the court. The court also stated that it was inappropriate for children of the ages of the children in this case to sign a formal document such as a deed of change of name.

In *Re C (A Minor) (Change of Surname)* [1998] 2 FLR 656, an unmarried couple separated when their child was aged 2. The child had been registered under her father's surname. The mother intended to change the child's surname. The father objected. The mother nevertheless changed the child's surname by deed poll. This came to light during the course of court proceedings issued by the father for parental responsibility and contact. The father then applied for a specific issue order, but by the time this application was heard the child was aged

5. Dismissing the father's application, the court held that the child's registered name was a matter of importance and changes could be justified only by the demands of welfare. As the mother was, at the time the name was changed, the only person with parental responsibility, the name had been changed lawfully. In those circumstances, the correct approach was to consider whether the original decision to change the name had been taken in the child's interests. On the facts, the mother's decision could not be justified, and her explanation that the child had a different surname at school or elsewhere, or that the father had refused to marry her, were irrelevant. There had, though, been an unfortunate delay in the matter being brought before the court and there was a risk, if the father's name was imposed, of its impacting upon contact. In those circumstances it was not considered in the interest of the child to order the use of the father's surname.

In *Dawson v Wearmouth* [1999] 2 AC 308, the House of Lords held that an order for a change of a child's registered name ought not to be made unless it can be shown to be justified and that it would be in the child's welfare. In his judgment Lord Jauncey said:

> A surname … given to a child at birth is not simply a name plucked out of the air (it) is a biological label that tells the world at large that the blood of the name flows in its veins. To suggest that a surname is unimportant because it can be changed at any time by deed poll when the child has attained more mature years ignores the importance of initially applying an appropriate label to that a child.

In *Re T (A Minor) (Change of Surname)* [1998] 2 FLR 620, the mother had three children by her estranged husband, when she met the father. Twins were born to the couple and they were registered in the father's name. The mother then separated from the twins' father. When the twins were aged 6, without consulting their father, the mother changed the twins' surname to that of her ex-husband with whom the twins had no connection at all. The mother's explanation was that it was more convenient for the children to have her former husband's name. On appeal, it was held that the children's names were an important issue and that in any situation the consent of the other parent or the court was essential. The court directed that the twins should revert to their father's name.

In *A v Y (Child's Surname)* [1999] 2 FLR 5, a child born to a married couple was registered in the mother's maiden name. The father took no action at the time because he was unaware of his right to do so. Shortly after the birth the parents separated. During proceedings for contact with the child the father applied for an order requiring that the child should use his name. At the date of the hearing the child was aged 4 and attending a nursery school. Applying the principles set out in s 1 of the Children Act 1989, the court found that the father's delay in this case was relevant as the child had become used to using her given name. To change her name would result in the child's having a name which was different from that used by other members of her household, and there was no benefit to the child in having the father's name added to her registered name and giving the child a double-barrelled name.

In *Re W (A Child) (Illegitimate Child: Change of Surname) sub nom Re W (A Child) (Change of Name); Re A (A Child) (Change of Name); Re B (Children) (Change of Name)* [2001] Fam 1, the Court of Appeal set out some of the factors or countervailing reasons which might be considered by a court. These included:

(a)   the reasons given for changing or seeking to change the name;

(b)   the fact that the child's name was or was not the same as that of the parent making the application would not generally carry much weight;

(c)   the reason for an earlier unilateral decision might be relevant;

(d)   any changes in the circumstances since the original decision might be relevant;

(e)   where the parents were married to each other the fact of the marriage was a strong factor;

(f)   the registered name of the child and the reason for the registration was relevant but not an all-important factor;

(g)   if the child was registered in the father's name there would have to be strong reasons to change the child's name, thus recognising the importance of the biological link;

(h)   where the parents were unmarried the degree of the father's commitment to the child and the quality of contact and the existence or absence of parental responsibility were relevant.

In *Re S (Change of Names: Cultural Factors)* [2001] 2 FLR 1005, a child born to a Muslim mother and a Sikh father bore three Sikh names. Following a divorce, the mother applied to change the child's name to a Muslim name on the ground that the Muslim community would never accept, socially and culturally, a child bearing a Sikh name. Allowing the mother's application, Wilson J found that for the child and his mother to be able to integrate into the obviously appropriate environment, the Muslim community, it was essential for the child to be known on a day-to-day basis by Muslim names and to be registered at school and with the health practice in that name, but there was no benefit to the child in changing his registered name formally by deed poll. There was a danger that a formal change of name could be seen by the child, when he grew older, as an elimination of his Sikh identity and as an endorsement of a desire to erase any reference to his Sikh identity.

In *Re R (A Child) (Surname: Using Both Parents)* [2001] EWCA Civ 1344, [2001] 2 FLR 1358, the mother of the child was Spanish and the father English. The mother intended to live with the child in Spain where the customs about naming a child were different from those in England, in that the child took on one of the maternal surnames and one of the paternal surnames. So combining the child's parents' surnames was considered a solution to bridge the divide between the parents. The court could not find any justification for a change to the mother's surname as the mother requested. The child was very young. The change in the name was not required to enable the mother to move to Spain; at the date of the hearing there was nothing in the mother's circumstances to suggest any certainty or permanency in her life. The burden was on her to justify the change and she had failed to discharge that burden.

In *Re X and Y (Leave to Remove from Jurisdiction: No Order Principle)* [2001] 2 FLR 118, a case under s 13(2) of the Children Act 1989 relating to removal of a child permanently from the jurisdiction, in determining the issues Munby J applied the welfare check list.

It will be observed from the above cases that, while the decision in any case will turn on the particular facts of that case, the burden of proof is on the party seeking to change the child's name to justify the change. In determining the application the child's welfare is always the court's paramount consideration. The cases suggest some of the factors which might be relevant in considering any application for a change of name.

The wishes of a child, while relevant, are not conclusive (see *W v A sub nom W v A (Child Surname)* [1981] Fam 14) but in *Re S (A Minor) (Change of Surname)* [1999] 1 FLR 672, a case relating to a child in the care of the local authority, it was held that in determining the issue of a change of name consideration must be given to the wishes and feelings needs and objectives of the child. The court should pay heed where the child has had the advantage of advice from a guardian ad litem who has had the opportunity to make a thorough investigation of the family dynamics. Searching scrutiny should be given to the motives and stated objectives of those opposing the change.

The objection of a non-resident parent is an important factor because the name provides a significant link between the child and the non-resident parent and the child's identity rights. The reason for the other parent's objection is also a relevant consideration, In *Re T (Otherwise H) (An Infant)* [1963] Ch 238, Buckley J said:

to deprive the child of his father's name, in my judgement is something which is not in the best interests of the child because, I think, it is injurious to the link between the father and the child to suggest to the child that there is some reason why it is thought desirable that she should be called by some name other than the father's name (see also *Re B (Change of Surname)* [1996] 1 FLR 791 and *Re T (A Minor) (Change of Surname)* [1998] 2 FLR 620, but see *A v Y (Child's Surname)* [1999] 2 FLR 5).

Cultural factors are also an important consideration (see *Re S (Change of Names: Cultural Factors)* [2001] 2 FLR 1005. In *Re A (Change of Name)* [2003], a Somali woman began a relationship with a Somali man and within 3 months of divorcing her husband conceived a child. On the child's birth she registered the child in her ex-husband's name. The father of the child sought an order that the boy should bear his name. At first instance he succeeded on the grounds that the Somali patrilineal naming principle required that the boy's second forename should be that of his father and his third name that of his paternal grandfather. The mother argued that she would lose dignity within her community if the child was given the name of the father. The Children and Family Reporter reported that the Imam of a mosque had advised that in Islamic law the child conceived by the mother within 4 months of her divorce should bear the name of the mother's ex-husband. No expert had been called at the hearing on this issue. At the appeal hearing two experts confirmed the father's position and one confirmed that under Islamic law a child conceived within 4 months of the divorce would be regarded as the husband's child and thus supported the mother's case regarding her social position within the community. The mother's appeal was allowed.

The Court of Appeal stressed that it was absolutely fundamental in Children Act proceedings that any expert report commissioned must be made available in the litigation even if it is contrary to the interests of the party who has commissioned it. That means that it must be disclosed to the other side. It must be disclosed to the court and it must be disclosed to any other expert approached.

3.7 Children in care

Section 33 (7) of the Children Act 1989 provides that while a care order is in force with respect to a child no person may cause the child to be known by a new surname.

When dealing with an application for a change of name in such circumstances, the case law concerning disputes between the child's parents may not be relied upon solely, as different considerations apply where the child is in care. In *Re S (A Minor) (Change of Surname)* [1999] 1 FLR 672, Thorpe LJ set out the following principles:

> In determining an application [to change the name of a child in care] by a *Gillick* competent child in the care of a local authority the welfare principle must of course be paramount. However, in addition the judge should give very careful consideration to the wishes, feelings, needs and objectives of the applicant. If he has the advantage of advice from a guardian ad litem who has had the opportunity to make a thorough investigation of the family dynamics he should pay particular heed. Next he must give searching scrutiny to the motives and stated objectives of the respondent.

See also *Re M, T, P, K and B (Care: Change of Name)* [2000] 2 FLR 45 where it was held that in any application to change a child's name, whether in public or private proceedings, the child's welfare was the paramount consideration and *Re S (A Minor) (Change of Surname)* [1999] 1 FLR 672.

3.7.1 Child who is a ward of court

The court's leave is required before any important steps are taken by any person who has the day-to-day care of a child who is a ward of court. Since the change of a child's name is an important decision the court's permission must be obtained before any change is made.

3.7.2 Adopted child

On the making of an adoption order, the adopters acquire all the rights and obligations of the child's natural parents and therefore have parental responsibility for the child. The natural parent's rights including parental responsibility are extinguished (s 46 of the Adoption and Children Act 2002). The adopters should apply for any change of name on the application for adoption so that the court when dealing with the application and on the making of an adoption order will also make an order for the child to be known by the new name.

3.7.3 Special guardianship order

Where a child is placed with a person(s) under a special guardianship order the person(s) acquire parental responsibility which they share with the birth parents but they are entitled to exercise parental responsibility to the exclusion of any other person with parental responsibility. However, they require the consent of those sharing parental responsibility with them in relation to any matter affecting the child or any rights which a parent of the child has in relation to the child's adoption or placement for adoption. They do not have the right to cause the child to be known by a new surname without the written consent of every person who has parental responsibility for the child or the leave of the court (s 14C of the Children Act 1989). Similar consideration will apply to any change of a child's forename (see below).

3.8 Changing a child's forename(s)

In relation, however, to forenames, different consideration may apply. In *Re H (Child's Name: First Name)* [2002] EWCA Civ 190, [2002] 1 FLR 973, the parents had separated when the mother was 6 weeks pregnant. They met again when the mother gave birth to their child to discuss the names that the child should be given but no agreement was reached. The father without the knowledge of the mother registered the child with his preferred names. The mother subsequently also registered the child with names of her choice. In determining the issue Thorpe LJ said:

> There are a number of points which should be made. The first is that none of the authorities that guide the court in determining disputes as to the surname by which a child should be known seem to be of any application to a dispute of this sort. The surname by which a child is registered and known is of particular significance insofar as it denotes the family to which the child belongs.

> Given names have a much less concrete character. It is commonplace for a child to receive statutory registration with one or more given names and, subsequently, to receive different given names, may be at baptism or, maybe, by custom and adoption. During the course of family life, as a child develops personality and individuality, parents or other members of the family, may be attracted to some nickname or some alternative given name which will then adhere, possibly for the rest of the child's life, or possibly only until the child's individuality and maturity allows it to make a choice for itself as to the name by which he or she wishes to be known.

> ...

> If issues such as this arise, it seems to me that judges must look in a worldly, common-sense way at what is likely to be best for the child and must not place too much emphasis upon the statutory process of registration ... Any search for the welfare of the child must in the end lead to the question what order was likely to promote a sense of security and well-being in the mother. The mother as a single parent and primary carer, requires a good deal of support both in the

outcome of legal proceedings and in the recognition of her liberty, matching her responsibility, to make decisions in the daily life of the child.

He also stated that it was clearly wrong to attempt to prevent the mother from using the names that she had chosen in dealings with external authorities and in the home. To inhibit the mother to the names given by the father would be unfair but it had to be recognised by her that the child had an immutable series of names by statutory registration.

3.8.1 Parents in same sex relationships or civil partners

The Civil Partnership Act 2004 has given equal status to those who enter civil partnerships as heterosexual couples who enter marriage.

The HFEA 2008 has made amendments to the Children Act 1989 to enable a second female in a same sex relationship to acquire parental responsibility and to the 1953 Act to enable her to be registered as a parent (see Chapter 2).

Section 2(1A) of the Children Act 1989 now provides that where a child:

(a)   has a parent by virtue of s 42 of the HFEA 2008, or

(b)   has a parent by virtue of s 43 of the HFEA 2008 and is a person to whom s 1(3) of the Family Law Reform Act 1987 applies,

the child's mother and the other parent shall each have parental responsibility for the child.

Section 2(2A) provides that where a child has a parent by virtue of s 43 of the HFEA 2008 and is not a person to whom s 1(3) of the Family Law Reform Act 1987 applies:

(a)   the mother shall have parental responsibility for the child;

(b)   the other parent shall have parental responsibility for the child if she has acquired it (and has not ceased to have it) in accordance with the provisions of this Act.

Section 4 of the Children Act 1989 has been amended by the insertion of a further subs 4ZA to make provision for the acquisition of parental responsibility by a second female parent. It provides:

> **4ZA** (1) Where a child has a parent by virtue of section 43 of the HFEA 2008 and is not a person to whom section 1(3) of the Family Law Reform Act 1987 applies, that parent shall acquire parental responsibility for the child if—

(a) she becomes registered as a parent of the child under any of the enactments specified in subsection (2);

(b) she and the child's mother make an agreement providing for her to have parental responsibility for the child; or

(c) the court on her application, orders that she shall have parental responsibility for the child.

...

(4) The agreement under section 1(b) is also a 'parental responsibility agreement' and section 4(2) applies in relation to such an agreement as it applies in relation to parental responsibility agreements under section 4.

(5) A person who has acquired parental responsibility under subsection (1) shall cease to have that responsibility only if the court so orders.

(6) The court may make an order under subsection (5) on the application:

(a) of any person who has parental responsibility for the child; or

(b) with the leave of the court, of the child himself, subject, in the case of parental responsibility acquired under subsection (1)(c) to section 12(4) (ie which restricts the right of the court to bring to an end the parental responsibility of any person while a residence order remains in force).

Section 12(1A) now provides that where the court makes a residence order in favour of a woman who is a parent of a child by virtue of s 43 of the HFEA 2008 it shall, if that woman would not otherwise have parental responsibility for the child, also make an order under s 4ZA giving her that responsibility. (amended by Sch. 6, para 28 HFEA 2008)

The HFEA 2008 makes further amendments to the Children Act 1989 to bring the status of women who are in same sex relationships on the same footing as those who have had a child from a heterosexual relationship. This includes the responsibility for the maintenance of the child and for applications to be made for financial provision for the child under Sch 1 to the Children Act 1989.

The Legitimacy Act 1976 has also been amended by the HFEA 2008 to provide for the legitimation of the child if the child's mother and the second female subsequently enter into a civil partnership.

However, it should be pointed out that where a lesbian couple have a child other than by anonymous gamete donation, difficulties can arise unless a clear written agreement is entered into with the known sperm donor. Whilst this may not oust the court's jurisdiction to consider any disputes that may arise, a written agreement, if made, would identify the intention of the parties at the time and assist the court in determining any dispute between the parties. The case of *Re M (Sperm Donor Father)* [2003] Fam Law 94 illustrates the problems which the parties to such an arrangement can face. In *Re M*, a married man agreed to father a child for a lesbian couple with the arrangement that he could act as a father figure for the child but with the lesbian couples being the primary carers and decision makers for the child. A dispute arose between them regarding the frequency of his visits and his involvement. On his application for contact and parental responsibility, the court granted the lesbian couple a joint residence order; made a defined contact order in favour of the father and adjourned his application for parental responsibility for further consideration after a period of contact had taken place.

In relation to male couples where a child is born as a result of a private surrogacy arrangement, the woman who carried the child is the child's mother and will have parental responsibility for the child and the person who fathered the child will have the same rights as any other heterosexual unmarried father. Hence the father can only have parental responsibility for the child and thereby be entitled to make decisions in relation to his child, which includes the decision to choose the name of his child or change it, if he is registered as the child's father (see Chapter 2). If not so registered he will not automatically acquire parental responsibility but in the absence of an agreement by the mother to sign a parental responsibility agreement he will have to apply under s 4 of the Children Act 1989 for an order and under s 8 for a specific issue order in relation to any dispute concerning the name of the child.

Given the difficulties that may arise, it is advisable where a woman agrees to be a surrogate mother to enter into a clear agreement. Whilst such an agreement or arrangement is not enforceable by or against the person making the arrangement and it is an offence to enter into such an agreement on a commercial basis, it will assist the court in its determination should any dispute arise. Where a child is born as a result of such an arrangement and is handed over to the father, if the father is in a same sex relationship or has entered into a civil partnership, in order for the male partner to be on an equal footing with the father it would be desirable for the father and his male partner to obtain a joint residence order and thus acquire parental responsibility. The child's name can then only be changed with the consent of both partners. Alternatively, they can apply to adopt the child. This is now possible under the provisions of the Adoption and Childen Act 2002. On the making of the adoption order they can apply for the child's forenames and surname to be changed to one of their choice.

In the further alternative, when s 54 of the HFEA 2008 comes into force (expected April 2010), civil partners and unmarried couples or same sex couples not in a civil partnership will be able to apply for a parental order. As in the case of adoption, on the making of the parental order the couple will be able to apply for the registered name of the child to be changed to one of their choice. The new regulations/rules relating to an application under s 54 have not as yet been finalised.

An application for a parental order asks the court to make an order permitting the applicant/s to treat the child in law as their child. The woman who carries the child cannot be one of the applicants.

The application for a parental order must be made by two people. The applicants may be married, civil partners, or heterosexual unmarried couples, same sex couples not in a civil partnership but who are living in an enduring family relationship and who are not within the prohibited degree of relationship to each other.

It should be noted that a limitation period applies to an application for a parental order. The application must be made within 6 months of the child's birth or in the case of applicants who were not able to apply under s 30 of the HFEA 1990, the application must be made within 6 months beginning from the date on which s 54 of the HFEA 2008 comes into force (expected April 2010) (s 54(11) of the HFEA 2008).

The Civil Partnership Act 2004 also provides that any civil partner in a civil partnership is entitled to apply for a residence order or a contact order specific issue and prohibited steps order.

3.9 Procedural tables

3.9.1 Application for parental responsibility order

Who may apply?	Father without parental responsibility	CA 1989, s 4(1)(a)
	The spouse or civil partner of a parent with parental responsibility	CA 1989, s 4A
Venue	Family proceedings court, county court and High Court Proceedings may be transferred upwards, downwards or horizontally	CA 1989, ss 10(1), 92(7); FPR 1991, r 2.40 C(AP)O 1991
The application	Free-standing in Form C1 with a copy for each respondent	FPR 1991, r 4.4(1)(a); FPC (CA 1989) R 1991, r 4(1)(a), Sch 1
Fee payable	£ 175	FPFO 2008, Fee 2.1
Respondents	Applicant must serve notice in Form C6 on every person with parental responsibility; if a care order is in force, on every person with parental responsibility before the care order	FPR 1991, r 4.7; FPC (CA 1989) R 1991, r 7, Sch 2
Other parties	Notice in Form C6 to be served on any person who has the care of the child, eg local authority; and on any other person joined by order of the court	FPR 1991, r 4.4; FPC (CA 1989) R 1991, r 4, Sch 2; FPR 1991, r 4.7; FPC (CA 1989) R 1991, r 7

Service of proceedings	Applicant must serve a copy of the application with Form C6 with notice of hearing endorsed thereon, on each respondent and any other party at least 14 days before the hearing	FPR 1991, r 4; FPC (CA 1989) R 1991, r 4, Sch 2
Acknowledgement	The recipient of Form C6 must complete and return Form C7 to the court and to all other parties within 14 days of receipt.	FPR 1991, rr 4, 4.9
Interlocutory hearings	The court will give directions, and timetable and/or transfer the proceedings	FPR 1991, r 4.14(2), (3); FPC (CA 1989) R 1991, r 14(2), (5), (6)
Final hearing	Make or refuse order conferring parental responsibility on the father	CA 1989, ss 4(1)(a), 12(1); FPR 1991, rr 4, 4.21; FPC (CA 1989) R 1991, r 21(7)(a)

3.9.2 Application for a specific issue order

Who may apply?	Parent or guardian; person with residence order; and person with leave	CA 1989, s 10
Venue	High Court, county court or family proceedings court	CA 1989, ss 10, 92(7); FPR 1991, r 2.40
The application	In Form C1 with a copy for each respondent	FPR 1991, r 4.4; FPC (CA 1989) R 1991, r 4
Fee payable	£ 175 unless exempted	FPFO 2008, Fee 2.1

Respondents	Notice to be served on every person with parental responsibility; local authority if caring for the child; any other person caring for the child; and any other party to pending proceedings	FPR 1991, rr 4.4, 4.7; FPC (CA 1989) R 1991, r 4
Service of proceedings	Unless time has been abridged, at least 14 days before hearing.	FPR 1991, r 4.4; FPC(CA 1989) R 1991, r 4
	Applicant must file proof of service	FPR 1991, r 4.8(7); FPC (CA 1989) R 1991, r 8(7)
Acknowledgement	Respondent must complete, file and serve Form C7	FPR 1991, r 4.9(1); FPC (CA 1989) R 1991, r 9
Interlocutory hearings	Court will give appropriate directions and timetable	FPR 1991, r 4.14(2), (3), (4); FPC (CA 1989) R 1991, r 14
Final hearing	Court will make appropriate specific issue order, or refuse to make an order	CA 1989 ss 8, 11(7); FPR 1991, r 4.21(5); FPC (CA 1989) R 1991, r 21(7)

Abbreviations used in the tables above:

C (AP)O 1991: Children (Allocation of Proceedings) Order 1991 (SI 1991/1677);

FPC (CA 1989) R 1991: Family Proceedings Courts (Children Act 1989) Rules 1991 (SI 1991/1395);

FPR 1991: Family Proceedings Rules 1991 (SI 1991/1247);

FPFO 2008: Family Proceedings Fees Order (SI 2008/1054).

3.9.3 Applications for a Parental Order under the Human Fertilisation and Embryology Act 2008

Proposed amendments to the Family Proceedings Court (Children Act 1989) Rules 1991 for parental orders will insert new rules 21A–21J and proposed amendments to the Family Proceedings Rules 1991 will insert a new Part IVA. The amendments will also make provision for parallel rules to be added into the new Family Proceedings Rules (which are intended to come into force in April 2011) by adding a new Part 12A. Some of the rules are modelled on FP(A)R 2005. The following Guide is provided, based on the draft rules, as a guide to practitioners but reference must be made to s 54 of the Act and the new rules, when they are issued and are in force, when future applications are contemplated.

Who may apply	Married heterosexual couples	HFEA s 54; FPC(CA1989)R 1991, r 21G(1), as amended; FPR 1991 r.4A.7, as amended
	Civil partners	
	Unmarried heterosexual couples living as partners in an enduring relationship	
	Same sex couples living as partners in an enduring relationship	
Which court	The proceedings must be commenced in the family proceedings court unless certain conditions set out in the ATPO apply, when it may be commenced in the High Court or county court	ATPO 2008, as amended
	Proceedings may be transferred upwards, sideways or downwards	ATPO 2008
Application	Freestanding in Form C51 for each child (if more than one) with sufficient copies for each respondent	FPC(CA 1989) R 1991, r 21D, as amended; FPR 1991, r.4A.4(1), (2), as amended

Documents to be filed with application	Marriage certificate if the applicants are married	FPC(CA 1989)R 1991, r 21D(3), as amended; FPR 1991, r 4A.4, as amended
	Civil partnership certificate if applicants are civil partners	
	Child's birth certificate	
	Any relevant orders	
Grounds for Application	Consent of the birth parent(s)	
	or birth parent(s) cannot be found	
	or birth parent(s) are incapable of giving consent	
Respondent	The birth parent(s)	FPC(CA 1989)R 1991, r 21G(1), as amended; FPR 1991, r 4A.7(1), as amended
	The child	
	Any person in whose favour there is provision for contact	
	Any other person or body with parental responsibility for the child	
	Any other person with parental responsibility on the direction of the court and on request by that person	FPC(CA 1989)R 1991, r 21G(2), (3)(*a*), as amended; FPR 1991, r.4A.7(2), (3)(*a*), as amended
	Any other person or body on the direction of the court	
Appointment of parental order reporter	As soon as is practicable after issue the court must appoint a parental order reporter	FPC(CA 1989)R 1991, r 21H(1) (*c*), as amended; FPR 1991, r 4A.8(*c*), as amended

Service	Copy of the application and supporting documents, notice of hearing and first direction hearing (Form C6) and Form C52 must be served on each respondent within 14 days before the hearing or first directions hearing; Form C6A must be served on any local authority or voluntary organisation who has accommodated the child	FPC(CA 1989) R 1991, r.21J, as amended; FPR 1991, r 4A.10, as amended
Acknowledgement	Each respondent must file and serve within 7 days of service in Form C52 on all other parties	FPC(CA 1989) R 1991, r 21JA, as amended; FPR 1991, r 4A.11, as amended
First direction hearing	Must take place within 4 weeks of issue of the application unless the court otherwise directs	FPC(CA 1989) R 1991, r 21JB, as amended; FPR 1991, r 4A.12, as amended
Directions	(*a*) Fix a timetable for: – parental order reporter's report – statement of fact or amendment to it – any other evidence (*b*) Directions relating to the parental order reporter's report and other evidence (*c*) Consider whether any other person should be made a party and give appropriate directions in relation thereto (*d*) Consider the appointment of a guardian ad litem or next friend for a protected person (*e*) Consider transfer of proceedings (*f*) Give direction for tracing the birth mother, service, disclosure and final hearing	FPC(CA 1989) R 1991, r 21JC, as amended; FPR 1991, r 4A.13, as amended

	May be given on Form A101 or a form to like effect	
	Any form of agreement executed in Scotland must be witnessed by a Justice of the Peace or sheriff	
	Any form of agreement executed in Northern Ireland must be witnessed by a Justice of the Peace	
Consent of birth parent(s)		FPC(CA 1989) R 1991, r 21JE, as amended; FPR 1991, r 4A.15, as amended
	Any form of agreement executed outside the UK must be witnessed by:	
	(*a*) any person currently authorised by law in the place where the document is executed to administer an oath for any judicial or other legal process	
	(*b*) a British Consular officer	
	(*c*) a notary public	
	(*d*) an officer holding a commission in any of the armed forces if the person executing the document is serving in the regular armed forces	
Disclosure of parental order reporter's report	Only on the direction of the court	FPC(CA 1989) R 1991, r 21JG, as amended; FPR 1991, r 4A.17), as amended
Notice of final hearing	Must be given in Form C6 by the court on the parties and the parental order reporter	FPC(CA 1989) R 1991, r 21JH, as amended; FPR 1991, r 4A.18, as amended

Final hearing	Any person who has been given notice of the hearing may attend and be heard on the question of whether an order should be made	FPC(CA 1989) R 1991, r 21JI, as amended; FPR 1991, r 4A.19, as amended
	The court may direct that any person may attend the hearing	
Order	A parental order takes effect on the date when it is made or such later date as the court may specify	FPC(CA 1989) R 1991, r 21JO, as amended; FPR 1991, r 4A.25, as amended
	If the proceedings are in Wales a party may request the order to be drawn up in Welsh as well as in English	

4 Change of Name by Deed Poll

4.1 Introduction

In England and Wales any adult person may legally change his or her name by simple assumption and usage so long as the intention in so doing is not fraudulent. Change by usage and reputation is the only way in which a name can be changed.

There is no legal requirement or procedure which needs to be adopted, save in the case of children, as set out in Chapter 3. Good examples of acquisition of a name by usage and reputation are the cases of *R v Billinghurst (Inhabitants)* (1814) 3 M & S 250 and *Dancer v Dancer* [1949] P 147.

A change of name by deed poll and by various other ways referred to later are merely ways of evidencing and advertising the change. In certain instances such evidence may be necessary; for example where a person is a member of a profession, the rules applicable to the governing body of the profession may require the change to be evidenced by deed poll or in some other way. In this chapter a change of name as evidenced by deed poll, and the enrolment of the deed, are discussed. The other ways of effecting the change are dealt with in Chapter 5.

4.2 The deed poll

The most common method of evidencing a change of name is by executing a deed poll and having it witnessed. Standard forms for this are obtainable from law stationers and specimen forms are set out at Appendix 2, Precedents 1 & 2.

Where it is intended to change a child's name by deed poll, the form differs depending on whether the child is aged under 16 or over 16. In the case of a child aged under 16, provided the parents agree, or one of them is dead or cannot be found, the change of name can be evidenced in the same way as by an adult executing a deed poll, but the deed is executed by the parent on behalf of the child.

Where the child is aged over 16, the child may execute the deed on his or her own behalf subject to the consent of the child's parents; or the deed may be executed by the parents on behalf of the child, but it must be endorsed with the child's consent. Specimen forms are shown at Appendix 2, Precedents 3 & 4.

When duly executed and attested, the deed may be enrolled in the Central Office of the Supreme Court. The conditions laid down in the Enrolment of Deeds (Change of Name) Regulations 1994 must be complied with (see below 4.3). There is no legal provision which requires that a deed poll of change of name must be enrolled. An application to enrol is entirely discretionary. The enrolment of a deed poll does not make the change of name any more legally effective than the execution of the deed itself. The purpose and advantages of enrolling the deed are that it provides certainty and safe custody; copies are available when required; and the change of name is advertised in the *London Gazette*. There is no time limit within which a deed poll may be enrolled.

A change of name which has been evidenced by a deed poll may be changed again by another deed, or by any other means whether formal or informal. A deed which has been enrolled may be cancelled. Where a dispute arises with respect to a change of name, for example between parents where a child's name has been changed by one parent unilaterally, as happened in *Re T (Otherwise H) (An Infant)* [1963] Ch 238, the court to which the application is made may declare that the deed was ineffective to change the name.

An alien is free to change his name like any other individual and may effect the change by deed poll or by any other means. If the change is effected by deed poll the deed may not, however, be enrolled because the regulations mentioned above require that the applicant must be a British citizen or a Commonwealth citizen as defined by s 37(1) of the British Nationality Act 1981 (BNA 1981).

4.3 Enrolment of a deed poll

The Enrolment of Deeds (Change of Name) Regulations 1994 came into operation on 1 April 1994, and provide as follows:

> 2. – (1) A person seeking to enrol a deed poll ('the applicant') must be a Commonwealth citizen as defined by section 37(1) of the BNA 1981.
>
> (2) If the applicant is a British citizen, a British Dependent Territories citizen or a British Overseas citizen, he must be described as such in the deed poll, which must also specify the section of the BNA 1981 under which the relevant citizenship was acquired.

(3) In any other case, the applicant must be described as a Commonwealth citizen.

(4) The applicant must be described in the deed poll as single, married, widowed or divorced.

3. – (1) As proof of citizenship named in the deed poll, the applicant must produce—

(a) a certificate of birth; or

(b) a certificate of citizenship by registration or naturalisation or otherwise; or

(c) some other document evidencing such citizenship.

(2) In addition to the documents set out in paragraph (1), an applicant who is married must–

(a) produce his certificate of marriage; and

(b) show that notice of his intention to apply for the enrolment of the deed poll has been given to his spouse by delivery or by post to his spouse's last known address; and

(c) show that he has obtained the consent of his spouse to the proposed change of name or that there is good reason why such consent should be dispensed with.

4. – (1) The deed poll and the documents referred to in regulation 3 must be exhibited to a statutory declaration by a Commonwealth citizen who is a householder in the United Kingdom and who must declare that he is such in the statutory declaration.

(2) The statutory declaration must state the period, which should ordinarily not be less than 10 years, during which the householder has known the applicant and must identify the applicant as the person referred to in the documents exhibited to the statutory declaration.

(3) Where the period mentioned in paragraph (2) is stated to be less than 10 years, the Master of the Rolls may in his absolute discretion decide whether to permit the deed poll to be enrolled and may require the applicant to provide more information before so deciding.

5. If the applicant is resident outside the United Kingdom, he must provide evidence that such residence is not intended to be permanent and the applicant may be required to produce a certificate by a solicitor as to the nature and probable duration of such residence.

6. The applicant must sign the deed poll in both his old and new names.

7. Upon enrolment the deed poll shall be advertised in the *London Gazette* by the clerk in charge for the time being of the Filing and Record Department at the Central Office of the Supreme Court.

4.4 Definitions

4.4.1 Commonwealth citizen

The Regulations require that the applicant must be a Commonwealth citizen within the meaning of s 37(1) of the BNA 1981. That section provides that:

Every person who—

(a) under the British Nationality Act 1981 is a British citizen, a British Dependent Territories citizen, a British national (Overseas), a British Overseas citizen or a British subject; or

(b) under any enactment for the time being in force in any country mentioned in Schedule 3 is a citizen of that country,

shall have the status of a Commonwealth citizen.

The countries listed in Sch 3 whose citizens are Commonwealth citizens are:

Antigua and Barbuda	Guyana
Australia	India
The Bahamas	Jamaica
Bangladesh	Kenya
Barbados	Kiribati
Belize	Lesotho
Botswana	Malawi
Brunei	Malaysia
Cameroon	Maldives
Canada	Malta
Republic of Cyprus	Mauritius
Dominica	Mozambique
Fiji	Namibia
The Gambia	Nauru
Ghana	New Zealand
Grenada	Nigeria

Pakistan	Sri Lanka
Papua New Guinea	Swaziland
Saint Christopher and Nevis	Tanzania
Saint Lucia	Tonga
Saint Vincent and the Grendadines	Trinidad and Tobago
	Tuvalu
Seychelles	Uganda
Sierra Leone	Vanuata
Singapore	Western Samoa
Solomon Islands	Zambia
South Africa	Zimbabwe

4.4.2 British citizen

British citizenship may be acquired in a number of ways under the BNA 1981.

By birth or adoption

Under s 1(1) of the BNA 1981 a child born in the United Kingdom after the commencement of the Act is a British citizen if, at the time of birth, the child's father or mother is a British citizen or settled in the United Kingdom. Note, however, that:

(i) a child born on a British aircraft or ship is a British citizen only if at least one of the parents was a British citizen at the time of his birth, or the child would, but for this provision, have been stateless (s 50(7));

(ii) a child born in the United Kingdom whose mother or father is a diplomat is not a British citizen;

(iii) a person is settled in the United Kingdom if ordinarily resident in the United Kingdom without being subject under the immigration laws to any restriction on the length of time for which he or she may remain (s 50(2)). No one who is in breach of the immigration laws can be said to be ordinarily resident in the United Kingdom. Therefore a child born to such a person does not qualify to acquire British citizenship under s 1(1) (s 50(5)).

By subsequent acquisition

A child born in the United Kingdom who did not acquire British citizenship at birth may acquire it subsequently by registration:

(i)   where either of his parents subsequently becomes a British citizen or becomes settled in the United Kingdom; the child is under the age of 18 years; and an application is made for the child's registration (s 1(3));

(ii)   if the child has remained in the United Kingdom for 10 years since birth without being absent for more than 90 days in any one year (s 1(4)). Where the child has remained absent for a period in excess of 90 days the Secretary of State has a discretion to disregard the excess (s 1(7));

(iii)   under Sch 2, para 3, which provides that a person born in the United Kingdom or a dependent territory after commencement of the BNA 1981 is entitled, on application for registration, to be registered if the following requirements are satisfied:

- the child is and always has been stateless; and

- on the date of the application the child has attained the age of 10 but is under the age of 21; and

- the child was in the United Kingdom or a dependent territory (no matter which) at the beginning of the period of 5 years ending with that date, and (subject to para 6) the number of days on which he was absent from both the United Kingdom and the dependent territory in that period does not exceed 450. In special circumstances the Secretary of State has discretion to disregard any excess (Sch 2, paras 3 and 6 of the BNA 1981).

If a child is stateless, then if either of his parents is a British Dependent Territories citizen, a British Overseas citizen or a British subject, the child acquires British citizenship (Sch 2, para 1 of the BNA 1981).

Where a child is adopted in the United Kingdom by a person who, at the date of the adoption, is a British citizen, the child acquires British citizenship. Where the adoption is by two persons jointly then it is sufficient if only one of the adopters is a British citizen. But if both or either of them are settled in the United Kingdom this does not confer British citizenship on the adopted child.

A newborn baby found abandoned in the United Kingdom acquires British citizenship (s 1(2)).

By descent

A person born outside the United Kingdom after the commencement of the BNA 1981 is a British citizen, if at the time of birth, the person's father or mother:

(i)   is a British citizen by birth, adoption, registration or naturalisation; or

(ii)   is a British citizen and is serving outside the United Kingdom in Crown Service, the recruitment for which took place in the United Kingdom; or

(iii)   is a British citizen and is serving outside the United Kingdom with any of the European Community institutions, the recruitment for which took place in any of the member states (s 2(1)).

By registration

British citizenship by registration may be acquired by a child, a person who is a British Dependent Territories citizen, a British Overseas citizen, a British subject under the BNA 1981 or a protected person. (For the relevant provisions see ss 3–5, 7–9, 15, 19, 20 and 22.)

By naturalisation

Application for naturalisation may be made only by a person of full age and capacity and subject to the requirements set out in Sch 3 (ss 6 and 18).

4.4.3 British Dependent Territories citizen

A person may acquire British Dependent Territories citizenship by birth, adoption, descent, registration and naturalisation. The requirements are similar to those applicable to acquisition of British citizenship. The relevant provisions are set out in ss 15–25 of the BNA 1981.

4.4.4 British overseas citizen

British overseas citizens are those who were citizens of the United Kingdom and Colonies who are not British citizens or British Dependent Territories citizens. Under the BNA 1981 this form of citizenship was not perpetuated and the number is diminishing. The relevant provisions are ss 26–28 of the BNA 1981.

4.4.5 British subject

The provisions are set out in ss 30–33 of the BNA 1981. British subjects are:

(i) persons who were British subjects without citizenship by virtue of s 13 or s 16 of the BNA 1981; or

(ii) alien women who had registered as British subjects under the British Nationality Act 1965;

(iii) certain former citizens of Eire who were British subjects prior to 1 January 1949.

Where the applicant is a British Dependent Territories citizen or British overseas citizen, not only must the person be described as such in the deed poll but the section of BNA 1981 under which the relevant citizenship was acquired must also be specified. In the case of Commonwealth citizens it is sufficient to refer to s 37(1) of the BNA 1981.

4.5 Affidavits and sworn statements

Regulation 3(2) of the Enrolment of Deeds (Change of Name) Regulations 1994 requires that, on enrolling the deed, where the applicant is married, the marriage certificate must be produced. Also it must be shown that notice of intention to change the name has been given to the other spouse by delivery or by post, and that the other spouse has consented to the application or that there are grounds for dispensing with such consent. Evidence of these matters should be given in an affidavit or sworn statement which should:

(a) set out the reason for the change of name;

(b) exhibit a copy of the marriage certificate;

(c) confirm that notice of the intention to apply for enrolment of the deed poll evidencing the change of name has been given to the other spouse, and state the manner in which such notice was given, ie by personal delivery or by post as the case may be;

(d) state whether the other spouse has consented, refused to consent or failed to consent;

(e) exhibit the form of consent if consent has been given;

(f) if it is intended to apply for consent to be dispensed with, include a specific application for such consent, setting out the grounds. If the ground is that the other spouse's whereabouts are not known, the affidavit or sworn statement must set out all the relevant details including when, where and in what circumstances he/she was last seen; the last known addresses of his/her residence and employment; details of family who may be able to assist in tracing the person; and the steps which have been undertaken to trace him or her;

(g)   if the applicant is living with another, set out the name of the cohabitee, and whether the person is married, separated or divorced;

(h)   if the applicant and/or the cohabitee have children from their relationship or from a previous marriage, include particulars of the children, ie their names, dates of birth, residence, and other relevant facts;

(i)   where relevant, evidence as required by reg 5, that the residence outside the United Kingdom is not intended to be permanent.

A sample form of affidavit seeking dispensation from the requirement of spouse's consent can be found at Appendix 2, Precedent 10.

4.6 Procedural steps

When the deed poll has been executed in the appropriate form, the executed deed should be presented to the Filing and Record Department at the Royal Courts of Justice, Strand, London WC2A 2LL. It must be accompanied, as appropriate, by passports, immigration documents, certificate of registration or naturalisation or other document evidencing citizenship, birth certificate, statutory declaration by the householder if appropriate (see Appendix 2 Precedent 5 for forms), any necessary consents and affidavits, a draft of the *London Gazette* advertisement, and two cheques or postal orders in respect of the fees in the appropriate sums.

A request for the fee is issued on acceptance of the documents, whereupon the appropriate fee should be paid and the request returned to the Department. The deed, endorsed with the certificate of enrolment and a copy of the relevant issue of the *London Gazette*, is forwarded by post to the applicant or the applicant's solicitors.

4.7 Change of a child's name by deed poll

4.7.1 The deed poll

A child's name may be changed by deed poll either:

(a)   by the parents if they agree; or

(b)   with the leave of the court (see Chapter 3).

Although not essential, the deed poll may be enrolled in the High Court. Regulation 8 of the Enrolment of Deeds (Change of Name) Regulations 1994 makes provision for the enrolment of deeds in respect of children. Enrolment does not give the deed any statutory force but it provides certainty, particularly regarding compliance with the relevant requirements, and safe custody; in addition, copies are easily available if later required.

In addition to the provisions of reg 8, the requirement for the consent of the other parent, on an application by a parent to change the name of a child by enrolment of a deed poll, is governed by a Practice Direction (see page 68), which supplements the regulations and must be read in conjunction with it.

Regulation 8 provides as follows:

(1) Subject to the following provisions of this regulation, these Regulations shall apply in relation to a deed poll evidencing the change of name of a child as if the child were the applicant.

(2) Paragraphs (3) to (8) shall not apply to a child who has attained the age of 16, is female and is married.

(3) If the child is under the age of 16, the deed poll must be executed by a person having parental responsibility for him.

(4) If the child has attained the age of 16, the deed poll must, except in the case of a person mentioned in paragraph (2), be executed by a person having parental responsibility for the child and be endorsed with the child's consent signed in both his old and new names duly witnessed.

(5) The application for enrolment must be supported—

(a) by an affidavit showing that the change of name is for the benefit of the child, and

(i) that the application is submitted by all persons having parental responsibility for the child; or

(ii) that it is submitted by one person having parental responsibility for the child with the consent of every other such person; or

(iii) that it is submitted by one person having parental responsibility for the child without the consent of every other such person, or by some other person whose name and capacity are given, for reasons set out in the affidavit; and

(b) by such other evidence, if any, as the Master of the Rolls may require in the particular circumstances of the case.

The provisions of reg 4(2) (see page 60) do not apply but the requirement for a statutory declaration from a householder does; it must state how long the householder has known the deponent and the child respectively. The requirement for the enrolment to be advertised in the *London Gazette* does not apply where the application is on behalf of a child under the age of 16.

The regulation specifically provides that the term 'parental responsibility' has the meaning given in s 3 of the Children Act 1989.

Practice Direction: Child: Change of Surname [1995] 1 WLR 365 (20 December 1994) provides as follows:

> 1. (a)   Where a person has by any order of the High Court, county court or family proceedings court been given parental responsibility for a child and applies to the Central Office, Filing Department, for the enrolment of a deed poll to change the surname (family name) of such a child who is under the age of 18 years (unless in the case of a female, she is married below that age), the application must be supported by the production of the consent in writing of every other person having parental responsibility.
>
> (b)   In the absence of such consent the application will be adjourned generally unless and until leave is given to change the surname of such child in the proceedings in which the said order was made and such leave is produced to the Central Office.
>
> 2. (a)   Where an application is made to the Central Office, Filing Department, by a person who has not been given parental responsibility for the child by any order of the High Court, county court or family proceedings court for the enrolment of a deed poll to change the surname of such child who is under the age of 18 years (unless in the case of a female, she is married below that age), leave of the court to enrol such a deed will be granted if consent in writing of every person having parental responsibility is produced or if the person (or, if more than one, persons) having parental responsibility is dead or overseas or despite the exercise of reasonable diligence it has not been possible to find him or her for other good reason.
>
> (b) In cases of doubt, the Senior Master or, in his absence, the Practice Master, will refer the matter to the Master of the Rolls.
>
> (c) In the absence of any of the conditions specified above, the Senior Master or the Master of the Rolls, as the case may be, may refer the matter to the Official Solicitor for investigation and report.

4.7.2 Consent

The Regulations and the Practice Direction, read in conjunction, clearly require that where there are no pending proceedings it is essential to obtain the written consent of the other parent; or to provide evidence to show that the other parent is dead, beyond the seas or, despite reasonable diligence, cannot be found; or that there is other good reason to dispense with consent.

4.7.3 Benefit of the child

As in the case of an application to the court for leave under reg 8(5)(a), the person wishing to change the child's name must show that the change is for the benefit of the child. Evidence to this effect must be submitted by affidavit and must be supported by such other evidence as may be required by the Master of the Rolls.

4.7.4 Child's age

In the case of a child aged under 16, the deed must be executed by the parents or person(s) having parental responsibility for the child. This includes the local authority where a care order is in place. Where the local authority is the applicant, the resolution by the local authority to change the child's name, and any other relevant circumstances in respect of the child which would show that it would be to the child's benefit to change his or her name, should be produced. The deed should be executed by an authorised local authority officer.

Where the child is over sixteen years of age:

(i)   the parent or person(s) with parental responsibility may execute the deed, but the child's consent must be endorsed on the deed and witnessed (reg 8(3)); or

(ii)   the child may execute his or her own deed, but the application to enrol it must be made by the parents, or person(s) with parental responsibility, and supported by affidavit.

In all cases, the householder's declaration must accompany the application.

Where a man intends to change his name and it is intended that the rest of the family should assume the same new name, it is desirable to include particulars of his wife and children in the deed, to show clearly that the change is intended to apply to them as well. Where a child is aged over 16, his or her consent must be endorsed on the deed.

5 Other Methods of Changing a Name

5.1 By reputation

A surname, in common law, is simply the name by which a person is generally known. If a person assumes a name, not for the purposes of fraud or deceit, but on a bona fide claim of right, a court of law has no power to control the action of such a person (*Cowley v Cowley* [1901] AC 450 at 458):

> An adult can change his or her name at any time by assuming a new name by any means as a result of which he or she becomes customarily addressed by the new name. There is no magic in a deed poll. The effect of changing a name by deed poll, as has been seen, is merely to record the change in solemn form which will perpetuate the evidence of the change of name. But a change of name on the part of an adult must, in my judgement, involve a conscious decision on the part of the adult that he wishes to change his name and be generally known by his new name. An infant ... is not competent to make such a decision. Certainly an infant of tender years cannot of its own motion change his or her surname. (per Buckley J in *Re T (Otherwise H) (An Infant)* [1963] Ch 238 at 240 and 241)

Thus there is no need to enter into any formal legal procedure so long as the person is identified by his or her assumed name.

There may, however, be circumstances, such as when applying for a passport, which require evidence of the acquisition of the new name by reputation to be produced. To facilitate and ease the change, various ways are employed to record it. Change by deed poll (see Chapter 4) is the most obvious method and the most commonly used, but there are others.

5.2 By advertisement

The change may be recorded by placing an advertisement in a local and/or national newspaper, renouncing the old name and recording the assumption of the new name. Frequently the advertisement is placed in the *London Gazette* (for a precedent see Appendix 2 Precedent 12).

5.3 By statutory declaration

The Statutory Declarations Act 1835 prescribes the form of declaration to be used. The declaration sets out the person's intention to change his or her name and records the intention to renounce, relinquish and abandon the old name and to adopt the new name. The declaration may be made before a person authorised to take oaths, or before a magistrates' clerk. A specimen form can be found at Appendix 2 Precedent 14.

5.4 By notarial instrument

Where it is required that a change of name be recognised worldwide, the change can be effected by a notarial act together with a declaration of the intention to renounce the original name and the intention to adopt the new name. The statutory declaration is prepared by a notary public. The declaration sets out the particulars of the person's citizenship, and then formally records the intention to renounce, relinquish and abandon the former name and to assume the new name. The declaration is made before the notary, who authenticates it and then records it in a register.

5.5 By marriage

On marriage it is usual for a woman to assume the surname of her husband, but it is not obligatory for her to do so. In recent years, with women entering the professions in increasing numbers, it is not uncommon for women to retain their maiden names.

Where, however, a woman on marriage has assumed her husband's name, she will continue to retain it unless she ceases to use it by reputation (see 5.1) and reverts to her maiden name or some other name (see *Cowley v Cowley* [1901] AC 450 and *Fendall v Goldsmid* (1877) 2 PD 263).

5.6 On confirmation

A Christian name given to a child on baptism may be changed on confirmation. The following passage from Coke's Institute 1.a (1633) is cited for this proposition: 'If a man be baptised by the name of Thomas, and after, at his confirmation by the bishop, he is named John, he may purchase by the name of his confirmation'. Coke mentions in that passage the case of Sir Francis Gawdie, Chief Justice of the Common Plea, who was given the name of Thomas on baptism but took the name of Francis on confirmation.

Dr Burn, in the ninth edition of his *Ecclesiastical Law* 80 questioned the accuracy of this view, but Phillimore (see *Ecclesiastical Law of the Church of England* (2nd edn, 1895), at 517) *was* of the opinion that the dictum remained good law. Phillimore mentions cases in which the precedent was followed, and there are also references in *Notes & Queries* 4th Series 6, 17 and 7 Series 2, 77.

In *Re Parrott* [1946] Ch 183 at 186, Vaisey J approved the opinion of Phillimore, and held that there were only three possible ways in which the name given on baptism could be changed, namely:

> ... first it may be assumed, by the omni-competence of an Act of Parliament as for example The Baines Name Act 1907. Secondly at confirmation as explained in Phillimore's *Ecclesiastical Law* ... A third method by which a Christian name may be in a sense altered is under the power to 'add' a name when the child is adopted; but the precise quality of such an added name is I think open to some doubt, for no one can in strictness possess more than one Christian name, whether it consists of one word or of several, and this method may perhaps be regarded as anomalous.

5.7 By Act of Parliament

A Christian name and surname may be changed by an Act of Parliament, such as the Baines Name Act 1907, a private Act under which the original Christian name Raymond Hill was changed to Henry Rodd. It is most unusual to use this method to change a name, but there may be instances where it is necessary to adopt it – for example, in the rare case where a will requires a change of name as a precondition of a gift. As to the procedure to be followed, see *Halsbury's Laws of England* (Butterworths Law, 4th edn, vol 34).

5.8 By Royal Licence

A name may be changed by Royal Licence. It is necessary to effect a change of surname in this way if a family intends to assume the arms of another family. An application must be made to the College of Arms for a petition in proper form to be drawn up by one of the officers of the arms and signed by the applicant. The application must state the grounds for the application and any other relevant matters. The application is submitted through the Secretary of State for the Home Department to the Sovereign.

The granting of the Royal Licence is discretionary. The Sovereign is advised by the Secretary of State, who obtains a report on the matter from the Garter King of Arms as representing the Earl Marshal (see further *Halsbury's Laws of England* (Butterworths Law, 4th edn, vol 35).

The Secretary of State will refer the petition to the Garter King of Arms representing the Earl Marshall for a report on the genealogical and heraldic aspects of the case. If the application is simply for a change of name it is likely that the application will be refused because a Royal Licence to effect a change of name is not necessary. Where the application relates to a transfer of arms to comply with a condition in a will, or is based on representation in blood traced through a maternal ancestor, it will be considered favourably. If there are no reasonable grounds for the application it will be rejected.

5.9 By deed poll recorded by the College of Arms

In addition to effecting a change of name by royal licence, the College of Arms also prepares and records changes of names by deed poll. The change of name is advertised in the *London Gazette*. The College keeps a record of the deed. It is not necessary for a deed prepared by the College to be enrolled at the Central Office. As in the case of enrolment, a deed recorded with the College has the advantage that it is in safe custody and copies can be obtained.

5.10 On adoption

On an application for an adoption order the applicants may apply for a change in the forenames of the child. If the application is granted the court directs that the child is to adopt a new name. A certified copy of the entry is entered on the Adopted Children's Register, and the original entry in the register of births is marked with the word 'adopted' or 're-adopted' or as the case may be (s 50 of the Adoption Act 1976, and similar provisions apply under s 77 of and Sch 1, para 1 to the Adoption and Children Act 2002, if the adoption is made under the 2002 Act).

6 Requirements of Some of the Professional Bodies

6.1 Introduction

A person who is a member of a professional or other organisation may be subject to special requirements for recording a change of name. Such requirements may be made by the governing body of the relevant organisation. The rules of some of the organisations are given in this chapter by way of illustration.

The recent tendency of the professional bodies, on an application for a change of name, is to accept a less formal approach than had previously been the case. In the case of organisations not mentioned in this chapter, less formal evidence may be adequate. It is suggested that where a person who is a member of a profession wishes to change his or her name, the relevant governing body should be contacted to ascertain the precise requirements which apply and the procedure to be adopted.

6.2 Solicitors

Pursuant to the Solicitors Act 1974, the Law Society maintains a roll in which is recorded the name by which a solicitor was known at the time of admission as a solicitor. Any change in the entry in the roll can be made in accordance with regulations made by the Master of the Rolls, with the concurrence of the Lord Chancellor and the Lord Chief Justice, under s 28 of the Solicitors Act 1974 as amended by s 8 of and Sch 1, para 8 to the Administration of Justice Act 1985. The applicable regulations are the Solicitors (Keeping of the Roll) Regulations 1989 . In place of the earlier, far more detailed provisions, reg 7 deals with an application for a change of name on the roll simply as follows: 'A solicitor whose name has changed may apply to change his or her name on the roll'.

The Regulations do not set out any particular method of making such an application. However, reg 12 provides that the Society may prescribe forms for applications to the Society, and in the case of an application under reg 7 it may require such evidence as it sees fit.

It is submitted that where the change of name is due to marriage, it would seem that a covering letter enclosing a certified copy of the marriage certificate will suffice. It is also suggested that where the change is for a personal reason, the application must be supported by some formal evidence of the change of name, such as a statutory declaration or deed poll.

Regulation 11 provides that the Society must confirm to the solicitor that his/her name has been changed on the roll, or if the application has been refused, give the solicitor notice of the refusal. Having regard to the provisions of the Human Rights Act 1998, the Society would be obliged to state the reasons for a refusal.

A person who is aggrieved by the Society's decision may appeal to the Master of the Rolls. Such appeals are governed by the Master of the Rolls (Appeals and Applications) Regulations 1991. The appeal must be made within 4 weeks of the Society's notifying the solicitor of the refusal (reg 14).

6.3 Opticians

The General Optical Council, established under the Opticians Act 1958, is responsible for maintaining registers of opticians. Entitlement to registration arises from achieving the appropriate qualification, and once qualified and registered, an optician may practise in the United Kingdom and some other countries.

Registration is governed by the General Optical Council (Registration and Enrolment Rules) Order in Council 1976 (now scheduled to the General Optical Council (Registration and Enrolment Rules) Order in Council 1977 SI 1977/176), which has been amended by subsequent Orders in Council, and which sets out the procedure. Rule 5 provides that each register must contain the full name, permanent address, practice address (es), qualification, registration number and date of registration. Application for registration is made on the appropriate form (r 8(1)), and the Council may require such further evidence in verification of the information given on the appropriate form as in its view is necessary to establish whether the applicant is entitled to be registered or enrolled (r 8(2)). A photograph with a signed certificate by someone who has known the applicant for 2 years confirming that the photograph is a true likeness of the applicant is also required. The application must include a declaration by the applicant that he has read, understood and will comply with the General Optical Council's Code of Conduct for individual restraints, and that he has understood the Council's right to use the information provided by the applicant to exercise its proper and statutory function.

Rule 10 provides for the register to be updated each year and for an annual fee to be paid. A form to update the information is sent to the optician annually, and if the optician wishes to remain on the register he or she must return the form completed with the relevant information and pay the requisite fee for the year; this must be done by 31 March each year. If the form is not returned and the fee is not paid the Council sends a reminder. If the optician fails to return the completed form and the fee within 14 days of the issue of the reminder the person's name is erased from the register.

Rule 12 provides that a registered optician must notify the Council, within one month, of any change in the particulars entered in the register relating to the optician's name, address or qualification. In the case of a change of name a photocopy of the the the change of name deed poll or in the case of a change of name by marriage or civil partnership a copy of the marriage certificate or civil partnership certificate should be enclosed. On receipt of the information the registrar must be satisfied that the information is correct. This is done by means of a statutory declaration or in some other appropriate form, for example, production of the deed poll or, where the change of name has occurred by reason of marriage, by requesting a certified copy of the marriage certificate.

6.4 Veterinary surgeons

The Veterinary Surgeons Act 1966 and the Veterinary Surgeons and the Veterinary Practitioners (Registration) Regulations Order in Council 1999 (SI 1999/2846) govern the profession. Section 2 of the Act requires the Council of the Royal College of Veterinary Surgeons to keep a register of its members. Under Sch 2, para 3 to the Order in Council the register must include the full name and any change of name of each person since registration; and the person's address, qualification, date of birth and registered index number. The application for registration is made on the appropriate form issued by the Council. An applicant for registration is required to send the form, together with evidence of his qualification and such other supporting evidence as the Council may require to establish whether the applicant is entitled to be registered (Sch 2, para 5).

A veterinary surgeon or veterinary practitioner must notify the registrar within one month of any change which affects the particulars entered in the register or supplementary veterinary register relating to his or her name or address (Sch 2, para 9).

Before altering the register the registrar may need to be satisfied, by a statutory declaration or by some other means, that the information is true, or the ground of the application is sufficient. In the case of a change of name by reason of marriage it will be necessary to submit a certified copy of the marriage certificate with the application. In other cases a statutory declaration of the change, or the deed poll, will be required. Whatever evidence is appropriate, the document must show the person's former name and the new name. The register is updated in a form which identifies and links the person in both names.

6.5 Medical practitioners

The registrar of the General Medical Council is required by law to keep a register containing the names, qualification, address and dates of registration of the persons registered in it and any other particulars as may be prescribed by regulations made by the General Medical Council. Under the Medical Practitioners Act 2008 all doctors are required to register with the General Medical Council. The original documents must be submitted to support the application. The doctor must also attend the General Medical Council's London Offices to undergo a pre-registration identity check. A photograph will then be taken and this will be made available to employers so they can be assured of the identity of the person concerned.

Alterations to a practitioner's registered name are governed by the Medical Practitioners' Registration (No 1) Regulations 1981. The relevant regulations are:

> 9. Subject to the provisions of regulation 10, when a fully or provisionally registered person applies to the Registrar to have an alteration made in his registered name, or notifies a change of address, or applies for the registration of an additional qualification, the Registrar shall, on being satisfied that it is correct to do so, alter the register in order to give effect to the application.

> 10. (1) A person who applies to have an alteration made in his or her registered name shall be required to satisfy the Registrar as to his or her identity. If the alteration results from marriage the person shall produce her marriage certificate or other official evidence of her marriage. In other cases, unless the alteration is insignificant, the Registrar may require a statutory declaration or other evidence of identity. Any questionable cases arising under this Regulation may be referred to the Registration Committee for determination.

> (2) On the insertion in the register of an alteration in the name of a person, the Registrar shall also retain in the register the name of the person as previously registered.

The originals of any documents required must be provided; photocopies may not be acceptable. A practitioner may also include with the application to register the change of name examples of both the former and the new signatures.

If a doctor wishes on a change of name for the new name to appear on the register or wishes to be registered in a different name to the one in which he/she is currently registered, he/she must make an application for this to be effected. The applicant will need to provide his/her original surname and forenames and the new surname and forenames, date of birth, contact details, telephone number, email address and set out the reasons for the change of name. If the change of name is due to marriage the original marriage certificate must be provided. In the case of a foreign marriage, if the certificate of marriage is in a foreign language, an official English translation or copy certified by the British Council or British Embassy must be submitted.

In the case of a female doctor who wishes to revert to her maiden name, the original old and new passport or original decree absolute or original birth certificate with an official translation if in a foreign language must be provided.

In the case of a change of name by the addition of a new first or middle name, the original old and new passport showing the names must be provided. Where there is a complete change of name the original new and old passport together with an explanation for the change of name must be provided even if these documents were submitted when the person first registered with the Council. Additional information may also be required.

Until registration is effected in the new name the applicant must continue to use his/her old name until confirmation is received that the change has been made to the register.

6.6 Dentists

The Dentists Act 1984 governs the practice and profession of dentistry. The profession is regulated by the dentists professional body, the General Dental Council.

Section 14 of the Dentists Act 1984 makes provision for the General Dental Council to keep a register of the names, qualifications, addresses and dates of registration of the persons registered in it. The Registrar appointed to keep the register may, when executing his duties, require and act upon such evidence as in each case appears sufficient (s 14(3)). A person seeking to be registered on the register must support the application by the document conferring or evidencing the applicant's licence or other qualification, and a statement of his/her name and address and other particulars (if any) required for registration (s 18(1) and (2)). Pursuant to s 19 of the Act the Council has authority to make regulations with respect to the form and keeping of the register and the making of entries in and erasures from the register. Section 25 provides that the registrar may insert any alteration in the name and address of any person so registered which comes to his knowledge. An entry in the register is admissible as evidence of all matters in it, on production of a certified copy (s 14(6)).

Application for an alteration in the register by reason of change of name must be made in written form, ie by letter or fax. In the case of a change by marriage the member must provide a certified copy of the marriage certificate. In all other cases the general policy is to require that a statutory declaration of the change witnessed by a solicitor, or a deed poll, is submitted.

6.7 Nurses and midwives

Nurses and midwives must notify any change of name to their governing body. The evidence required is similar to that outlined above.

6.8 Accountants

Members of the Institute of Chartered Accounts are governed by the regulations set out in its Members Handbook. Regulation 1.115(3) requires the associate to provide the Members' Registrar with particulars of his/her full names, his/her registered address, and any other address to which he/she elects to have correspondence sent.

Annually, the member is obliged to complete and return a questionnaire recording any change in the information previously provided.

Additionally, a member is obliged to inform the Members' Registrar of any change or changes to the information previously provided within 28 days from any such change or changes taking effect, and provide any other information reasonably required.

Although the regulations do not specifically set out the evidence which would be required to support an application for a change of name, it is submitted that in the case of a change by marriage a copy of the marriage certificate would need to be submitted; in any other case, a statutory declaration, deed poll or some other evidence would be required to show that the previous name has been universally abandoned and the new name assumed. Such evidence might consist of an advertisement in the *London Gazette*, or the fact that the new name is shown on the passport or recorded by other official agencies such as the Inland Revenue.

As to the names and letterheads of practising firms, the latter often consisting of the names of the individual partners, the Institute's guidelines are set out in reg 1.212 of the Members Handbook.

6.9 Chartered surveyors

The Royal Institute of Chartered Surveyors' guidelines governing the practice for recording a change of name is that, except in the case of marriage or divorce, a member who wishes to record a change of name, and/or obtain a diploma in a new name, must furnish evidence of having changed his or her name by deed poll.

In the case of a change by marriage or divorce, less formal notification is acceptable. In such cases the Institute requires the member to support the application with a copy of the marriage certificate, or, in the case of a divorce, a certified copy of the decree of divorce.

The member pays the costs of preparing the new diploma, and must return the old diploma to the Institute.

6.10 Architects

The standard procedure of the Architects Registration Council of the United Kingdom is that when a person completes an application to come on to the register in the first place, the applicant provides three security checks – date of birth, place of birth and signature. If at some subsequent date the architect notifies the Council of a change of name, he or she will need to provide a signature in the old name and the new name and confirm his/her date and place of birth. These particulars are then checked with the original information provided to the Council.

All changes of name must be reported in writing with a copy of the relevant official document, eg the marriage certificate or deed poll. The change must be reported by post, fax, email or via the Architects Registration Council website. The Architects Act 1997 provides that the Register shall show the regular business address of each registered person. Architects are registered as individuals, therefore any amendments to their registration detail must come from the individual alone. The Institute will not accept notification of any change from a third party, eg a friend or family member, colleague or any other professional body.

7 Effects of Changing a Name

7.1 Introduction

Once a person changes his or her name, provided it is not done for any fraudulent purpose, the new name may be used for all purposes.

7.2 Marriage banns

When a person who has changed his or her name intends to marry, the banns may be published in the assumed name (see *Dancer v Dancer* [1949] P 147 and s 8 of the Marriage Act 1949).

7.3 Legal proceedings

In any legal proceedings a person who has changed his or her name must claim and defend in the new name. If the name is changed during the course of the proceedings, the court and all other parties to the proceedings must be notified; the action will continue in the new name but with all the documents recording the former name of the person in parentheses. An order to this effect is generally not required.

Under the Civil Procedure Rules 1998, r 17.4(3), the court may give permission to amend the proceedings so as to correct the name of a party where there is no reasonable doubt as to the identity of the party intending to make a claim or against whom a claim is intended.

Furthermore, under r 19.2 the court may give permission to correct a mistake as to parties so long as it is genuine and no injustice is caused thereby, particularly where the identity of the party concerned is not in dispute and the amendment is sought only to state the party's correct name.

In a contractual situation a change of name may have the effect of frustrating a contract on the ground of mistaken identity if the effect is to negate consent. In the context of criminal law, if the change of name results in deception, the change of name may not provide a defence.

7.4 Driving licences

A person holding a current driving licence must immediately notify the Driver and Vehicle Licensing Authority (DVLA) at Swansea SA99 1BN of any change in his/her name or surname (Road Traffic Act 1988 and the regulations thereunder).

The DVLA will require a completed D1 application form for a driving licence together with the original of the document which confirms the new name (eg the deed poll or certificate of marriage) and the photocard driving licence and paper counterpart. The D1 application form may be obtained from any main Post Office or a request may be made to the DVLA form ordering service for the form to be sent by post.

Where the holder of the licence has only a paper driving licence, in addition to the completed D1 application form and the original document confirming the change of name, the DVLA will require a passport size photograph and the paper driving licence to be submitted.

The completed application form with all the relevant documents should be sent to DVLA, Swansea SA99 1BN.

7.5 Passports, state benefits and others

In the case of a change of name by marriage, a copy of the marriage certificate should be produced to the Passport Office along with the application to amend the details in the passport. In the case of a civil partnership if one of the partners wishes to adopt the surname of his/her partner, the civil partnership certificate should be accepted. Where the couple wish to take a double barreled surname documentary evidence of a change to the double-barrelled name will need to be provided, eg a deed poll. Another option may be for one of the couple to use his or her surname as an additional forename/middle name. In this instance the change must be made by deed poll. Where the couple decide to take on a completely new surname this must be done be deed poll by both of them. The same applies to notifying the Benefits Agency. It is also important to notify any other relevant organisation, for example the bank or other financial institution, of the change of name.

Where on separation from his/her partner a person wishes to revert to his/her previous name, the change should be effected by deed poll as documentary evidence of the change. This will become necessary if the person wishes the details on his/her passport, or other documents to be altered.

Where the marriage or the civil partnership has terminated by divorce or dissolution of the civil partnership the decree absolute or the dissolution of the civil partnership certificate will suffice for most purposes.

In the event of a change by adoption, or by any other order of court, a certified copy of the order should be sent with the application. Where the change of name has been effected by any other method, a copy of the deed poll, statutory declaration, notarial instrument, advertisement in the press, certificate of record from the College of Arms, special Act of Parliament, or as the case may be, will need to be provided.

On a change of name by reputation, a letter from a professionally qualified person such as a doctor, lawyer, minister of religion, Member of Parliament or justice of the peace, who has known the applicant in both names, testifying that the change has been effected for all purposes, may be acceptable. Even in such a case, however, it would be simpler and easier to execute a deed poll.

In the case of a child whose parents are married to each other, in the absence of any objection made to the Passport Office, a passport will be issued to a child on the consent of either parent. Where the child's parents have not been married to each other, the consent of the mother alone is relevant as she is usually the only person with parental responsibility. Where the father has acquired parental responsibility, whether by agreement or order of court, he is able to intervene. For changes in the unmarried father's rights and that of a step-parent to acquire parental responsibility, see Chapter 3. Where the child's name has been changed, a passport in the new name is issued only if the application is accompanied by a deed poll properly executed; or, in the case of an adopted child, by a copy of the adoption order; or, in any other case, by a court order permitting the change.

7.6 Company directors and shareholders

Section 10 of and Sch 1 to the Companies Act 1985 require that, before the incorporation of a company, the former and current names and surnames of the directors and secretary must be sent to the Registrar of Companies. Any alteration in the names of these individuals must be notified to the registrar of companies within 14 days of the change occurring (s 288 of the Companies Act 1985).

Every company is also required to keep at its registered office a register of its directors and secretaries and set out therein the particulars referred to in ss 289 and 290 relating to each individual. This includes the present name and any former name of each individual.

Shareholders are also required to notify the secretary of the company of any changes in their names. The company secretary should be contacted to ascertain what evidence is required to effect the change on the register of shareholders.

7.7 Limited liability partnerships

Under the Limited Liability Partnership Act 2000, 'name' in relation to a member of a limited liability partnership if an individual means his forename and surname, or in the case of a peer or other person usually known by a title, his title instead of or in addition to either or both his forename a nd surname.

By Section 9 of the Act a limited liability partnership must ensure that:

(a)   where a person becomes or ceases to be a member or designated member, notice must be delivered to the registrar within 14 days;

(b)   where there is a change in the name and address of a member, notice must be delivered to the registrar within 28 days;

The notice must be in a form approved by the registrar and must be signed by the designated member of the limited liability partnership or authenticated in a manner approved by the registrar. Failure to comply is an offence liable on summary conviction to a fine not exceeding Level 5 on the standard scale.

There are many other situations where it is necessary to provide evidence of the change of name. The nature of the evidence required varies, but in most instances a statutory declaration, a deed poll or some other legal document such as a court order, is desired.

Appendix One
Forms

Forms 1 to 6B are prescribed by the Registration of Births and Deaths Regulations 1987 (SI 1987/2088) as amended by the Registration of Births and Deaths (Amendment) Regulations 1994 (SI 1994/1948) and the Registration of Births and Deaths (Amendment) (England and Wales) Regulations 2009 (SI 2009/2165).

FORM 1   Particulars of Birth

http://www.opsi.gov.uk/si/si2009/uksi_20092165_en_2#sch1

FORM 2   Declaration/Statement for the Registration/Re-Registration of a Birth

http://www.opsi.gov.uk/si/si2009/uksi_20092165_en_2#sch1

FORM 3   Certificate that Name was Given in Baptism

http://www.opsi.gov.uk/si/si1987/Uksi_19872088_en_18.htm

FORM 4   Certificate that Name was Given otherwise than in Baptism

http://www.opsi.gov.uk/si/si1987/Uksi_19872088_en_18.htm

FORM 5   Statement for the Re-Registration of a Birth

http://www.opsi.gov.uk/si/si1987/Uksi_19872088_en_18.htm

FORM 6A   Declaration by Parent on Request for the Registration of a Birth

http://www.opsi.gov.uk/si/si2009/uksi_20092165_en_2#sch1

FORM 6B   Declaration by Parent on Request for the Re-Registration of a Birth

http://www.opsi.gov.uk/si/si2009/uksi_20092165_en_2#sch1

HFEA PP FORM

Your Consent to being the Legal Parent

http://www.hfea.gov.uk/docs/HFEA_PP_form.pdf

HFEA WP FORM

Your Consent to your Partner being the Legal Parent

http://www.hfea.gov.uk/docs/HFEA_WP_form.pdf

STANDARD ELECTION FORM

Mother's Election for the Father's Particulars to be Recorded in the Birth Register

http://www.hfea.gov.uk/docs/deceased_father_register_as_guidance.pdf

Appendix Two
Precedents

(1) DEED OF CHANGE OF NAME (FOR ENROLMENT)

This precedent can be adapted for change of forename (s).

THIS CHANGE OF NAME DEED intended to be enrolled at the Central Office, Royal Courts of Justice, Strand, London WC2A 2LL made this ...... day of .... Two thousand and ...... by me the undersigned JAMES WORTHY [bachelor] [spinster] [single] [married] [divorced] [woman] [widow] [widower] of .... (state address) now or formerly called or known as JAMES RAGBONE

[a British citizen by birth] or

[a British Dependent Territories citizen as defined by section ...... of the British Nationality Act 1981] or

[a British Overseas citizen as defined by section ...... of the British

Nationality Act 1981] or

[a Commonwealth citizen as defined by section 37 (1) of the British

Nationality Act 1981]

WITNESSES and IT IS HEREBY DECLARED as follows:–

1.   I absolutely and entirely renounce relinquish and abandon the use of my former surname of RAGBONE ('former surname') and assume adopt and determine to take and use from the date hereof the surname of WORTHY ('new surname') in substitution for my former surname of RAGBONE.

2.   I shall at all times hereafter in all records deeds documents and other writings and in all actions and proceedings as well as in all dealings and transactions and on all occasions whatsoever use and subscribe the new surname.

3.   I authorise and require all persons at all times to identify describe and address me by my new surname.

IN WITNESS whereof I have hereunto subscribed my former surname of RAGBONE and my new and assumed surname of WORTHYl on the aforesaid date.

SIGNED as a DEED by the above-named JAMES WORTHY formerly known as JAMES RAGBONE in the presence of:

Name: ....

Address: ....

Occupation: ....

Name: ....

Address: ....

Occupation: ....

(2) DEED OF CHANGE OF NAME (NOT FOR ENROLMENT)

THIS CHANGE OF NAME DEED made this ...... day of .... Two thousand and .... by me the undersigned JAMES WORTHY [bachelor] [spinster] [single] [married] [divorced] [woman] [widow] [widower] of ....

.... (state address) now or formerly called or known as JAMES RAGBONE

WITNESSES and IT IS HEREBY DECLARED as follows:–

1.   I absolutely and entirely renounce relinquish and abandon the use of my former surname of RAGBONE ('former surname') and assume adopt and determine to take and use from the date hereof the surname of WORTHY ('new surname') in substitution for my former surname of RAGBONE.

2.   I shall at all times hereafter in all records deeds documents and other writings and in all actions and proceedings as well as in all dealings and transactions and on all occasions whatsoever use and subscribe the new surname in substitution for my former surname to the intent that I may hereafter be called known and identified by the new surname instead of my former surname.

3.   I authorise and require all persons at all times to identify describe and address me by my new surname.

SIGNED as a DEED by the above-named JAMES WORTHY formerly known as JAMES RAGBONE in the presence of:

Name: ....

Address: ....

Occupation: ....

Name: ....

Address: ....

Occupation: ....

(3) DEED OF CHANGE OF NAME MADE ON BEHALF OF A CHILD (NOT FOR ENROLMENT)

This form can be used to change a forename, surname or both, but in the case of a baptismal forename, see 3.8 and 5.6.

THIS CHANGE OF NAME DEED made this ...... day of .... Two thousand and .... by [me] [us] the undersigned JACK JONES (name of parent or parents) of .... (set out the address in full) on behalf of [my] [our] [child] [son] [daughter] ANTHONY JONES now or formerly called ANTHONY SMELLIE

WITNESSES and IT IS HEREBY DECLARED as follows:–

1. On behalf of my said [child] [son] [daughter] [I] [we] absolutely and entirely renounce relinquish and abandon the use of [his] [her] former [forename] [surname] [forename and surname] of SMELLIE ('former surname') and assume adopt and determine to take and use from the date hereof the surname of JONES ('new surname') in substitution.

2. On behalf of my said [child] [son] [daughter] [I] [we] shall at all times hereafter in all records deeds documents and other writings and in all actions and proceedings as well as in all dealings and transactions and on all occasions whatsoever use and subscribe the new [forename] [surname] [forename and surname] in substitution for [his] [her] former [forename] [surname] [forename and surname] so relinquished as aforesaid to the intent that [he] [she] may hereafter be known and identified by [his] [her] new [forename] [surname] [forename and surname] and not by [his] [her] former [forename] [surname] [forename and surname].

3. [I] [We] authorise and require all persons at all times to designate describe and address [my] [our] said [child] [son] [daughter] by the new [forename] [surname] [forename and surname].

SIGNED as a DEED by the said JACK JONES on behalf of [his] [her] above-named [child] [son] [daughter] in the presence of:

Name: ....

Address: ....

Occupation: ....

Name: ....

Address: ....

Occupation: ....

(4) DEED OF CHANGE OF NAME MADE ON BEHALF OF A CHILD UNDER SIXTEEN (FOR ENROLMENT)

This form can be used to change a forename, surname or both, but in the case of a baptismal forename, see 3.8 and 5.6.

THIS CHANGE OF NAME DEED intended to be enrolled at the Central Office, Royal Courts of Justice, Strand, London WC2A 2LL made this .... day of .... Two thousand and ...... by [me] [us] the undersigned .... (name of parent or parents) of .... (set out the address in full) [single] [married] [divorced] [woman] [widow] [widower] on behalf of [my] [our] [child] [son] [daughter] ANTHONY JONES now or formerly called ANTHONY SMELLIE of .... who is seven years of age and is [a British citizen by birth] or [a British Dependent Territories citizen as defined by section .... of the British Nationality Act 1981] or [a British Overseas citizen as defined by section .... of the British Nationality Act 1981] or [a Commonwealth citizen as defined by section 37 (1) of the British Nationality Act 1981].

WITNESSES and IT IS HEREBY DECLARED as follows:–

1.   On behalf of my said [child] [son] [daughter] .... (insert full new name) [I] [we] absolutely and entirely renounce and relinquish and abandon the use of [his] [her] former [forename] [surname] [forename and surname] of SMELLIE ('former surname') and assume adopt and determine to take and use from the date hereof the surname of JONES ('new surname') in substitution.

2.   On behalf of my said [child] [son] [daughter] [I] [we] shall at all times hereafter in all records deeds documents and other writings and in all actions and proceedings as well as in all dealings and transactions and on all occasions whatsoever use and subscribe the new [forename] [surname] [forename and surname] in substitution for [his] [her] former [forename] [surname] [forename and surname] so relinquished as aforesaid to the intent that [he] [she] may hereafter be known and identified by [his] [her] new [forename] [surname] [forename and surname] and not by [his] [her] former [forename] [surname] [forename and surname].

3.   [I] [We] authorise and require all persons at all times to designate describe and address [my] [our] said [child] [son] [daughter] by the new [forename] [surname] [forename and surname].

SIGNED as a DEED by the said JACK JONES on behalf of [his] [her] above-named [child] [son] [daughter] in the presence of:

Name: ....

Address: ....

Occupation: ....

Name: ....

Address: ....

Occupation: ....

(5) STATUTORY DECLARATION IN SUPPORT OF CHANGE OF NAME DEED

I, ... of .... do solemnly and sincerely declare as follows:–

1. I am a Commonwealth citizen and a householder resident in the United Kingdom at the aforesaid address.

2. I have known the applicant .... (insert new name in full) formerly known as .... (insert former name in full) for a period in excess of ten years since about ....

3. There is now produced and shown to me marked 'A' a Change of Name Deed executed by the applicant on the ...... day of .... 20 .... I identify the applicant .... (insert new name) with the person named in the said Deed,

4. There is also produced and shown to me marked 'B' the following documents of the applicant .... (insert new name) formerly known as .... (insert former name in full):–

[(i) a certified copy of [his] [her] birth certificate];

[(ii) a certificate of [his] [her] citizenship by [registration] [naturalisation]];

[(iii) a certified copy of [his] [her] marriage certificate];

[(iv) the notice of intention sent to [his] [her] spouse and the consent of the spouse]];

[(v) the affidavit in support of the applicant's application].

The said .... (insert new name in full) referred to in said Deed and in the above-mentioned documents as .... (insert former name in full) is one and the same person.

5. I make this declaration from my personal knowledge of .... formerly known as ....

6. I make this solemn declaration conscientiously believing the same to be true and by virtue of the Statutory Declarations Act 1835.

Declared by the above-named ....

at ....

this .... day of .... 20 .....

Before me,

A Commissioner for Oaths/Solicitor.

(6) STATUTORY DECLARATION IN SUPPORT OF DEED CHANGING THE NAME OF A CHILD

I, ... of .... do solemnly and sincerely declare as follows:–

1.   I am a Commonwealth citizen and a householder resident in the United Kingdom at the aforesaid address.

2.   I have known .... formerly known as ...., a child, for a period in excess of ten years [since his birth on ....] [since ....].

I have known the child's [mother] [father] [mother and father] for a period of .... years since about ....

3.   There is now produced and shown to me marked 'A' a Change of Name Deed executed by the said child's [father] [mother] .... on the ...... day of .... 20 .... I identify the person .... with the person named in the said Deed.

4.   There are also produced and shown to me marked 'B' the following documents of the said .... formerly known as ....:–

[(i)   a certified copy of [his] [her] birth certificate];

[(ii)   a certificate of [his] [her] citizenship by [registration] [naturalisation]];

[(iii)   [his] [her] consent (where the child is sixteen years of age or over)];

[(iv)   the consent to [his] [her] [mother] [father]];

[(v)   the affidavit in support of [his] [her] [mother] [father]].

The said .... (insert new name in full) referred to in the said Deed and in the above-mentioned documents as .... (insert former name in full) is one and the same person.

5.   I make this declaration from my personal knowledge of .... formerly known as ....

6.   I make this solemn declaration conscientiously believing the same to be true and by virtue of the Statutory Declarations Act 1835.

Declared by the above-named ....

at ....

this .... day of .... 20 .....

Before me,

A Commissioner for Oaths/Solicitor.

(7) CONSENT OF SPOUSE TO ENROLMENT OF CHANGE OF NAME DEED

I, MARY RAGBONE of .... the wife of JAMES RAGBONE of .... make oath and say as follows:–

1.   JAMES RAGBONE has given me notice of his intention to apply for the enrolment of the Change of Name Deed a copy whereof is now produced and shown to me marked 'A' whereby he has now assumed the name of JAMES WORTHY instead of JAMES RAGBONE.

2.   I consent to the said change of name and to the enrolment of the said Deed at the Central Office, Royal Courts of Justice, Strand, London WC2A 2LL.

Sworn by the said MARY RAGBONE

at ....

this .... day of .... 20 .....

Before me,

A Commissioner for Oaths/Solicitor.

(8) CONSENT OF WIFE AND MOTHER WHERE HUSBAND EXECUTES A FAMILY DEED

I, ... of .... am the wife of .... formerly .... and the mother of the children referred to in the Change of Name Deed attached hereto.

I hereby consent to the change of name as set out in the said Deed in respect of myself and my children, and to the enrolment of the Deed at the Central Office, Royal Courts of Justice, Strand, London WC2A 2LL.

Signed ....

in the presence of

Name: ....

Address: ....

Occupation: ....

Name: ....

Address: ....

Occupation: ....

(9) CONSENT OF A CHILD OVER SIXTEEN TO CHANGE OF NAME BY DEED

I, ... of ....
.... am seventeen years of age, having been born on the ...... day of
....

I have read and approved the contents of the Change of Name
Deed dated .... witnessed and declared by my [father]
[mother] [parents]. I agree to the change of my name from ....
.... to .... and to the
enrolment of the said Deed at the Central Office, Royal Courts of
Justice, Strand, London WC2A 2LL.

Signed ....

formerly known as ....

in the presence of:

Name: ....

Address: ....

Occupation: ....

Name: ....

Address: ....

Occupation: ....

(10) AFFIDAVIT BY MARRIED WOMAN SEEKING DISPENSATION FROM REQUIREMENT FOR HUSBAND'S CONSENT TO A CHANGE OF NAME BY DEED

I, ... formerly known as ....
.... of ...., married woman, make oath
and say as follows:–

1. I was married to .... on the ...... day of ....
20 ..... at the Register Office in the District of .... in the
County of .... (as on marriage certificate). My maiden
name was .... I was then ...... years old, having been
born on the ...... day of .... 19....... .

2. There are no children of our marriage.

3. On the 1st of January 2000 I changed my name by deed poll
from .... to .... I now wish to enrol
the change of name deed and am informed by ....
and verily believe that I require my husband's consent so to do.

4. I make this affidavit in support of my application to dispense
with his consent.

5. I last lived with my husband at .... in 1960
when he left me. I have had no contact with him since then, nor have
I been aware of his whereabouts.

6. There are no relatives or friends of my husband who are now
known to me through whom I could trace him.

7. My husband was unemployed when we parted. He had no
bank account or other account as far as I am aware.

8. To the best of my knowledge and belief he was not a member
of a trades union or other professional organisation through which I
may be able to trace him.

9. On the ...... day of .... 20...... my solicitors wrote to the
Department of Social Security Special Records Section in Newcastle-
upon-Tyne to ascertain whether the Department was aware of his
whereabouts. A copy of the letter received is now shown to me marked
'A'. They do not have an address for him.

10. I know of no other inquiry that I can make to trace my husband.

11.   Since .... I have been cohabiting with
.... and have assumed his name.

12.   The said .... is a married man, living apart from
his wife. He has three children all of whom are adults.

Sworn by the said ....

at ....

this .... day of .... 20 .....

Before me,

A Commissioner for Oaths/Solicitor.

(11) AFFIDAVIT THAT CHANGE OF NAME OF A CHILD IS FOR THE BENEFIT OF THE CHILD

I, ... of .... make oath and say as follows:–

1.   I am the mother of .... and make this affidavit in support of my application to change the child's name from .... to ....

2.   I was married to .... on the ...... day of .... 20 .... The said .... was born on the ...... day of .... 20 .... She is the only child of our marriage.

3.   On the ...... day of .... 20 ...... my husband left me and on the ...... day of .... 20 ...... we were divorced. There is now produced and shown to me marked 'A' a copy of the decree.

4.   Thereafter my former husband went to Nicaragua and failed to communicate with me. I have tried to trace him through the Nicaraguan Embassy but to no avail.

5.   In .... I went to live with .... who is divorced. He has four children namely .... aged .... He has parental responsibility for his four children and a residence order. We have lived together as one family, and are regarded in the neighbourhood as such.

6.   My daughter .... attends the same school as the said four children.

7.   By a change of name deed executed by me on the ...... day of .... 20 ...... I have assumed the name of .... I wish my daughter to assume the same surname and have executed a deed on her behalf which I wish to be enrolled in the Central Office.

8.   All efforts to trace her father have proved unsuccessful. I know of no other steps which I could take to trace him.

9.   The said .... also wishes my daughter to assume his surname.

10.   In the premises I respectfully submit it would be in the interest and to the benefit of my daughter to be known by the same surname as myself and my cohabitee and his children whom she regards as her father and siblings respectively.

11.   At present she is registered at school in the name of
.... This has caused considerable curiosity among the
children and has resulted in my daughter being subjected to teasing
and unkindness from other children. This has caused her extreme
unhappiness and distress. There is now produced and shown to me
marked 'B' a report from the head teacher which is self-explanatory.

12.   In the circumstances I respectfully ask that there be leave to
enrol the change of name deed.

Sworn by the said ....

at ....

this .... day of .... 20 .....

Before me,

A Commissioner for Oaths/Solicitor.

(12) ADVERTISEMENT OF CHANGE OF NAME BY DEED FOR PUBLICATION IN THE LONDON GAZETTE

I hereby give notice that by a Deed Poll dated the ...... day of .... 20 ...... and enrolled at the Central Office, Royal Courts of Justice, Strand, London WC2A 1LL, I .... (insert new name) of .... [single] [married] [divorced] [a widow] [a widower] [a British citizen] [a British Dependent Territories citizen] [a British Overseas citizen] [a Commonwealth citizen] renounced relinquished and abandoned the name of .... and assumed the name of ....

Dated the .... day of .... 20 ....

(13) ADVERTISEMENT OF CHANGE OF NAME OF A CHILD BY DEED FOR PUBLICATION IN THE LONDON GAZETTE

I hereby give notice that by a Deed Poll dated the ...... day of ....
20 ...... and enrolled at the Central Office, Royal Courts of Justice, Strand, London WC2A 1LL, I, ... of ....
.... the [mother] [father] [mother and father] of ....
(insert new name in full) [an unmarried child] and [a British citizen] [a British Dependent Territories citizen] [a British Overseas citizen] [a Commonwealth citizen] renounced relinquished and abandoned the name of .... and assumed the name of
....

Dated the .... day of .... 20 ....

(14) STATUTORY DECLARATION EFFECTING CHANGE OF NAME

I, JAMES WORTHY, the deponent referred to in the Schedule hereto formerly known as JAMES RAGBONE being a British citizen by birth (or as the case may be) do solemnly and sincerely declare as follows:–

1.   I absolutely and entirely renounce relinquish and abandon the use of my former name as specified in the Schedule hereto ('my former name') and assume adopt and determine to take and use from the date hereof the new name specified in the said Schedule ('my new name') in substitution for my former name.

2.   I shall at all times hereafter in all records deeds documents and other writings and in all actions and proceedings as well as in all dealings and transactions and on all occasions whatsoever use and subscribe my new name in substitution for my former name so relinquished as aforesaid to the intent that I may hereafter be called known and identified by my new name and not by my former name.

3.   I authorise and require all persons at all times to identify describe and address me by my new name.

I make this solemn declaration conscientiously believing the same to be true and pursuant to the provisions of the Statutory Declarations Act 1835.

THE SCHEDULE

Former name: JAMES RAGBONE

New name: JAMES WORTHY

Address: ....

Occupation: ....

Declared by the above-named JAMES WORTHY

formerly known as JAMES RAGBONE

at ....

this .... day of .... 20 ....

Before me, ...

A Commissioner for Oaths/Solicitor.

(15) STATUTORY DECLARATION EFFECTING CHANGE OF NAME OF A CHILD

[I] [We], ... the deponent referred to in the Schedule hereto, the [mother] [father] [mother and father] of .... of ....

(set out address) do solemnly and sincerely declare as follows:–

1.   On behalf of [my] [our] [child] [son] [daughter] ....
.... now or formerly called .... [I] [we] absolutely and entirely renounce relinquish and abandon the use of [his] [her] former [forename] [surname] as specified in the Schedule hereto ('[his] [her] former [forename] [surname]') and assume adopt and determine to take and use from the date hereof the new [forename] [surname] specified in the said Schedule ('new [forename] [surname]') in substitution for [his] [her] former [forename] [surname].

2.   On behalf of [my] [our] said [child] [son] [daughter] [I] [we] shall at all times hereafter in all records deeds documents and other writings and in all actions and proceedings as well as in all dealings and transactions and on all occasions whatsoever use and subscribe the new [forename] [surname] of .... in substitution for [his] [her] former [forename] [surname] of .... so relinquished as aforesaid and to the intent that [he] [she] may hereafter be called known and identified by [his] [her] new [forename] [surname] and not by [his] [her] former [forename] [surname].

3.   On behalf of [my] [our] said [child] [son] [daughter] [I] [we] authorise and require all persons at all times to identify describe and address [him] [her] by [his] [her] new name.

I make this solemn declaration conscientiously believing the same to be true and pursuant to the provisions of the Statutory Declarations Act 1835.

THE SCHEDULE

Former [forename] [surname]: ....

New [forename] [surname]: ....

Address: ....

Declared by the above-named deponent[s] ....
.... on behalf of [his] [her] [their] [child] [son] [daughter] .... (new name)

at ....

this .... day of .... 20 ....

Before me, ...

A Commissioner for Oaths/Solicitor.

(16) STATUTORY DECLARATION FOR A CHANGE OF NAME ON GENDER REASSIGNMENT

STATUTORY DECLARATION

I, *Ruby Brown* of 13 Crooked Close Bordertown DO SOLEMNLY AND SINCERELY DECLARE as follows:

1. I, in pursuance for the fact that I am undergoing treatment to reassign my gender from [female] to [male] do absolutely and entirely renounce relinquish and abandon the use of my former names of *Ruby Brown* and assume adopt and determine to take and use the names of *Basil Paddy Brown*.

2. I shall at all times hereafter in all records deeds documents and other writings and in all actions proceedings as well as in all dealings and transactions on all occasions whatsoever use and subscribe the said names of *Basil Paddy Brown* as my name in substitution for the former name of *Ruby Brown* so relinquished as aforesaid to the intent that I may hereafter be called known or distinguished not by my former names of *Ruby Brown* but by the names of *Basil Paddy Brown* only.

3. I authorise and require all persons at all times to designate describe and address me by the adopted names of *Basil Paddy Brown*.

4. AND I make this Solemn Declaration conscientiously believing the same to be true by virtue of the provisions of the Statutory Declaration Act 1835.

SIGNED AND DECLARED at

[set out the address]

In the County of........ *[where a copy of the original is provided certfiy*

this.......day the ....of......2009 I hereby certify that this a true and complete

Before me ....   copy of the original

Solicitor   ....[*signature of Solicitor]*

   Solicitor

Statutory Declaration for a Change of Surname

STATUTORY DECLARATION

I.........*[former surname]* Mahoney of ....*[address and occupation]* DO SOLEMNLY AND SINCERELY DECLARE that:

I absolutely and entirely renounce and relinquish and abandon the use of my former surname of *Mahoney* and assume adopt and determine to take and use form the date hereof the surname of *McManus* in substitution of my surname of *Mahoney*.

I shall at all times hereafter in al records and proceedings as well as in all dealings and transactions on all occasions whatsoever use and subscribe the said name of *McManus* as my surname in substitution for my former surname of *Mahoney* so relinquished as aforesaid to the intent that I may hereafter be called known or distinguished not by my former surname of *Mahoney* but by the surname of *McManus* only.

I authorise and require all persons at all times to designate describe and address me by the adopted surname of *McManus*.

AND I make this Solemn Dec;aration conscientiously believing the same to e true and by virtue of the Statutory Declaration Act 1835.

Declared at ....[*address*] ....[*declarant's new signature*]

This .... Day of........2009

Before me

..........[*witness's signature*] .... [*declarant's former signature*]

Solicitor [*occupation*]